Living in the Anointing

Living in the Anointing

Tony Wastall

How to sustain a supernatural lifestyle
and fruitful ministry

Introduction

The anointing of the Holy Spirit is a power unlike anything else on earth. The greatest works of human strength do not even come close to what God can achieve through one touch of His Holy Spirit. Even passionate prayers, fasting and devotion to God's word, wonderful though they are, should not be confused with the anointing itself. One single demonstration of the Holy Spirit's activity outweighs the best human efforts every time.

God makes this clear to the prophet Zechariah when he is feeling overwhelmed by the daunting challenges the Jewish people face in rebuilding the temple in Jerusalem. They are a small returning remnant, surrounded by enemies and attempting the impossible. While Zechariah is wrestling with these issues God gives him a vision of the menorah, the seven branched lampstand that once stood in the temple. Two olive trees stand one either side of the lampstand, feeding fresh oil directly into its seven branches. Here is what we read:

> *Now the angel who talked with me came back and wakened me, as a man who is wakened out of his sleep. And he said to me, "What do you see?" So I said, "I am looking, and there is a lampstand of solid gold with a bowl on top of it, and on the stand seven lamps with seven pipes to the seven lamps. Two olive trees are by it, one at the right of the bowl and the*

> *other at its left." So I answered and spoke to the angel who talked with me, saying, "What are these, my lord?" Then the angel who talked with me answered and said to me, "Do you not know what these are?" And I said, "No, my lord." So he answered and said to me: "This is the word of the LORD to Zerubbabel:* ***Not by might nor by power, but by My Spirit,' Says the LORD of hosts.*** *'Who are you, O great mountain? Before Zerubbabel you shall become a plain! And he shall bring forth the capstone with shouts of "Grace, grace to it!" ' "*
>
> Zechariah 4:1-7

The mountain that stood in the path of completing the temple would be moved by the provision of fresh oil coming from the two olive trees, the anointing of the Holy Spirit. Whatever mountain may stand in the way of God's purposes in the earth, whatever challenges God's people face doing his will – it is all answered in this one statement;

> *'Not by might, not by power, but by my Spirit' says the Lord of hosts.'*
>
> (verse 6)

The purpose of God accelerates and the glory of God is revealed when the anointing is present. Devils know it and tremble. The enemies of God are confused. Strongholds are demolished. The kingdom of God advances in leaps and bounds.

There is something other worldly when someone operates in the anointing. No force of man or power of demons can withstand them because to do so is to oppose almighty God himself. When you truly realise what is possible through the anointing of the Holy Spirit you will covet it above anything else in your life. You will never consent to a substitute. You will not be fooled with a forgery. Once you have tasted the real thing, there is no going back.

We need the Holy Spirit as never before. The church faces enemies that can only be overcome by the power of heaven. The arm of flesh is powerless to defeat demonic ideologies, hostile governments or rampant secularism. Many churches and ministries do great works in the world today and we thank God for them all. Great things can be achieved by well-intentioned and prayerful activity carried out in the name of Christ. But there is a manifestation of God's power that eclipses all such efforts and of which we have seen only the beginning. God's prescription has not changed; '*"Not by might nor by power, but by My Spirit" says the Lord*'. In his book on this subject R T Kendall says, 'Next to the gift of salvation . . . the anointing is our most precious possession'. [1]

The anointing of the Holy Spirit will do one of two things. The anointing sets a person free or equips them to set others free. The Holy Spirit is the liberator and the empowerer. First of all God sent the Holy Spirit into the world to set people free! The apostle Paul says, 'Now the Lord is the Spirit; and where the Spirit of the Lord is, there is liberty', (2 Corinthians 3:17). The Holy Spirit is the bondage breaker and the emancipator. The prophet Isaiah put it like this:

> *It shall come to pass in that day that his burden will be taken away from your shoulder, and his yoke from your neck, and the yoke will be destroyed because of the anointing oil.*
>
> Isaiah 10:27

But secondly, the Spirit of God comes on a person to equip them to be God's instrumEnt of liberation. Bill Johnson often

1. R T Kendall, The Anointing, page 13

says, 'The Holy Spirit lives *in you* for yourself, but rests *on you* for others'. The anointing of the Holy Spirit turns captives into conquerors and sinners into sons. Those who were bound in darkness become instruments of righteousness.

The ultimate purpose of God is for the Holy Spirit to liberate and empower at the same time. This was the case for me when I was baptized with the Spirit at the age of sixteen. I was a very insecure and defeated young Christian. I was so hungry for God that night, I didn't even have time to argue myself out of his blessings. Shame, fear and compromise fell off me and in their place came love, joy and peace. I was transformed from the inside out.

But God did not simply leave me as a liberated believer. The anointing that came on me that night to set me free, remained on me with commissioning power to set others free. Along with a group of friends, I was launched into anointed ministry, preaching the gospel, praying for the sick and exercising the gifts of the Spirit.

The anointing should not be confused with other human or even divine activities. For example, the call of God is not the same thing as the anointing. Rather, the anointing is an empowered call. Natural gifting is not the anointing. But God can clothe natural ability with his anointing and super-charge it. A ministry is not the same as an anointing but a ministry can and should be operated in the power of the anointing.

The anointing is superior to everything. First of all it offers supernatural protection. When the people of Israel trekked the wilderness, humanly vulnerable to all their enemies, God declared over them, 'Do not touch my anointed ones, and do my prophets no harm' (Psalm 105:15). The anointing marked them and surrounded them as a shield and it is no different in our day. The anointing acts as a wall of fire around God's people.

Secondly, the anointing is the source of wisdom and counsel for the people of God. John says, 'You have an anointing from the Holy One and you know all things' (1 John 2:20). Of course John is not saying we are omniscient like God – but rather, the anointing teaches us whatever we need to know and as much as we need to know in any given situation! He keeps us from error and leads us into all truth. John expresses it further in the chapter in this way;

> *But the anointing which you have received from Him abides in you, and you do not need that anyone teach you; but as the same anointing teaches you concerning all things, and is true, and is not a lie, and just as it has taught you, you will abide in Him.*
>
> 1 John 2:27

But finally and more than anything else, the anointing empowers the church to continue the ministry of Christ in the earth. That is the subject of this book. Jesus said:

> *'. . . you shall receive power when the Holy Spirit has come upon you; and you shall be witnesses to Me in Jerusalem, and in all Judea and Samaria, and to the end of the earth.'*
>
> Acts 1:8

God's great cosmic plan of redemption – the advance of his kingdom in the lives of men and women – it will not slip or stumble; it will not falter or fail. Since the Day of Pentecost the anointing of the Holy Spirit has been unleashed and is at work in the world to ensure this.

The anointing of the Holy Spirit has been a hot topic for some years in the body of Christ. Inspiring books have been written on this subject and many amazing messages have been spoken on it. We must not however, become over familiar with something so precious and powerful. We dare not live in the after-glow of a previous generation's revelation and experience. There is a greater need than ever to both understand and embrace this gift of God to men and women. We need fresh oil today.

We will begin by gaining an understanding of what the anointing really is, we will look at the Bible passages and explore God's word so we really know what we are letting ourselves in for in seeking an anointed life. Then we are going to look at the personal side of the anointing and discover practical principles for living in the supernatural and protecting what we carry. Get your heart ready and have your Bible to hand. You are about to experience acceleration.

1

The Baptism with the Holy Spirit

The room was crowded with teenagers from my church youth group. We sat in a circle listening to the missionary who was sharing his story of pioneer evangelism and church planting in the jungles of Brazil. I had never come across anyone like this in my life. His eyes were bright, his face was alive with joy and he spoke with a conviction I had not encountered before.

His name was Gordon Emmens and the stories he told that night made our jaws drop. He and his wife Jacqui literally trekked from town to town through difficult jungle terrain, preaching the gospel to people who practiced a mixture of Catholicism and tribal religion. They healed the sick, cast out demons and even raised the dead. Sometimes they were forced to drink contaminated water from the jungle, so they prayed over it in Jesus' name, drank it and suffered no ill effects. At times they encountered hostile mobs seeking to drive them away. But God warned them, sometimes with an audible voice, and they escaped with their lives on more than one occasion.

Having told us his story Gordon went on to share the secret of this brand of victorious, faith-filled Christianity – the Baptism with the Holy Spirit. Until that night I had never even heard of the Baptism with the Holy Spirit. I knew the difference between dry formal Christianity and a real relationship with God. But this was something else. The clue to seeing God work miracles, heal the sick and deliver the oppressed – it was the Baptism with the Spirit. I drank in every word like a thirsty man finding an oasis in the desert. I was ready for all the Lord had for me. I needed no persuasion.

One by one we were invited to sit on a chair in the middle of the room while Gordon and the host of the meeting prayed for us. What happened next was about to change my life beyond recognition.

You must be born again

That year was 1971. I was sixteen years old and the Charismatic Movement was in full swing. It was a season in the life of the church when God was pouring out his Spirit on people from the historic denominations like Anglican, Methodist, Baptist and even Roman Catholic. The 19th Century had begun with Holy Spirit outpourings like that of the 1904 Welsh Revival and the 1906 Azousa Street revival in Los Angeles. These made way for the emergence of Pentecostal denominations like Assemblies of God, Church of Christ, Elim and many others. But the Pentecostal experience did not cross into mainstream Christianity until the 1960's when the Holy Spirit broke out in a fresh wave that came to be known as the Charismatic Movement.

Believers across the world were now discovering the distinct experience of Holy Spirit Baptism along with the gifts of the Holy Spirit like speaking in tongues, prophecy and healing. A few historic churches welcomed this new phenomena but on the whole it was rejected and this in turn gave rise to multitudes of Charismatic believers leaving their churches. However, instead of finding their way to the Pentecostal denominations, they began gathering in homes for worship, prayer and fellowship. In this way a spontaneous home church movement began.

By the early 1970's these massive shifts in the church landscape were sending shock waves through every denomination. The way people were 'doing church' was changing. New worship songs sprang up, capturing the historic moment. New personalities became household names and new church streams and networks emerged. I had no idea that as a 16 year old, with little knowledge or experience of the things of God, I would be caught up in this whirlwind of Holy Spirit activity.

I was born in Southend on Sea, Essex but at the age of just five years old, my family moved across country to a sleepy village in rural Somerset. My parents were Church of England by affiliation and my mother was a devout church attender, ensuring that I went to Sunday School along with my two sisters. I was twelve years old and attending High School when I first heard the gospel. My class was visited by a vicar named Dudley Carter who shared in very simple terms, the truth of salvation through faith in Jesus Christ. I sat there riveted by his words. The Holy Spirit seemed to be targeting my tender heart and I came under a powerful conviction of my sin and my need of a saviour.

That same night, alone in my bedroom, I knelt by my bed and prayed the sinner's prayer. With no-one to guide me and very little understanding beyond what I had heard earlier in the day, I more or less stumbled into the arms of my heavenly father. The following night I prayed again, and the night after that, until I was sure the Lord had heard me! My journey as a fully-fledged born-again Christian had begun.

Two other events took place that ensured I would grow in my new-found faith. The Gideon Bible Association visited our school and I received my first Bible, a New Testament and Psalms in the King James Version. Secondly, into our isolated village came a new Rector to the local Church of England church. His name was Joe Coffee and along with his wife Ann and his teenage son and daughter, he initiated a wonderful work of God in the Quantock Hills.

The Reverend Joe was a soundly born again businessman who had received a call into ministry mid-life and was now taking up his first ministerial appointment. The Coffees began a youth work. They opened their home for Bible Studies and Sunday night praise and fellowship times. It was all quite amazing. Word spread and within a matter of months a genuine work of the Holy Spirit was taking place in St Margaret's Church Spaxton. People began coming to the church from a wide area. Young and old gave their lives to Christ and I began to grow in my faith.

Wonderful though this was, I remained a very weak and insecure Christian. I was walking with one foot in the kingdom of God and one foot in the world – not a pleasant experience! By the age of 16 I was confused and frustrated. I genuinely loved the Lord but seemed powerless to live out the faith I claimed to follow and was deeply influenced by non-Christian friends. All that was about to change however.

My father had been head-hunted by his previous employer in Essex and in the summer of 1971 we relocated back to Southend on Sea. This was my opportunity for a new start. I prayed a simple but desperate prayer. 'Lord, I am going to break with my old life and my old friends. Please guide me and show yourself to me when I arrive in Southend. I offer myself to you afresh'. I had no idea how wonderfully God was going to answer that prayer.

I began attending the local Baptist Church and soon made new Christian friends. At my new school I met more genuine believers. Within a few weeks of joining the Baptist Church, the youth group was invited to go and listen to a visiting missionary speaker by the name of Gordon Emmens in the home of a man called Nobby Noble in the neighbouring town of Thundersley. At the time I had no idea what a life-changing moment that night would prove to be.

Power from on high

The evening arrived and as my youth group listened to the speaker we were given the opportunity to receive the Holy Spirit. One by one we were prayed for and soon it was my turn. I sat on the hot seat in the middle of the room and the two men placed their hands on my head and began to pray. Immediately I felt as though my body was on fire, not with pain but a presence I could not describe. My head, hands and feet began to tingle and vibrate. I instinctively stood to my feet, raised my arms in the air and opened my mouth to praise God. But from my lips came a language I did not recognise. I began to speak praises to God in other tongues, just as the early church did on the Day of Pentecost.

This experience continued for some minutes until I took my seat in the circle again and others were prayed for. It was a remarkable evening by any measure, all of us received from God without fully understanding what had taken place. For the second time in my life I found myself plunged into a God-encounter, this time I had become a Pentecostal, Charismatic believer and everything in my life was about to change again.

The fruit of my encounter with the Holy Spirit was immediate. First of all I fell in love with the word of God and found to my surprise I could understand it. Secondly, I discovered joy and peace for the first time – a confidence and certainty enveloped me. Finally, I became zealous for the Lord to use me. I wanted to share my faith, and for God to work through me in any way he could in order to see people come to know Christ. All of this sprung from my Baptism with the

Holy Spirit. I wanted to study it more deeply and understand all I could about this supernatural power and anointing from heaven.

My group of friends and I were gripped with a burning desire to share the gospel. We began meeting in the town centre on Saturdays to worship God, preach the gospel and talk to whoever would listen to us. We also opened a Coffee Bar called The Den, where every Saturday evening we conducted our evangelistic work. This continued for several years before the Lord led me step at a time, deeper into Christian ministry and leadership. A life-time of serving Christ began with an initiation into the anointing – the Baptism with the Spirit.

Biblical Basis

With my new-found love for God's word, I was curious to know more about my experience and so began searching the Scriptures and reading what others had to say on the subject. I was also blessed to sit under the ministry of many Charismatic leaders and preachers who travelled the country at that time, teaching on the Baptism and gifts of the Holy Spirit.

The first thing I discovered is that the Baptism with the Holy Spirit was thoroughly biblical. It was not simply a subjective experience with dubious credentials. It was rooted in Scripture. John the Baptist first made this announcement when preparing the way for Jesus:

> *John answered, saying to all, "I indeed baptize you with water; but one mightier than I is coming, whose sandal strap I am not worthy to loose. He will baptize you with the Holy Spirit and fire".*
>
> Luke 3:16

Then prior to his departure to the Father, Jesus tells his disciples to wait in Jerusalem for this very same experience of Holy Spirit Baptism:

And being assembled together with them, He commanded them not to depart from Jerusalem, but to wait for the Promise of the Father, "which," He said, "you have heard from me; for John truly baptized with water, but you shall be baptized with the Holy Spirit not many days from now."

Acts 1:4-5

This took place on the Day of Pentecost when the disciples were gathering and waiting as Jesus had instructed them.

When the Day of Pentecost had fully come, they were all with one accord in one place. And suddenly there came a sound from heaven, as of a rushing mighty wind, and it filled the whole house where they were sitting. Then there appeared to them divided tongues, as of fire, and one sat upon each of them. And they were all filled with the Holy Spirit and began to speak with other tongues, as the Spirit gave them utterance.

Acts 2:1-4

I discovered that this experience of the Holy Spirit is distinct from spiritual new birth. When Jesus appeared to his disciples, just risen from the dead, John records what happened;

So Jesus said to them again, "Peace to you! As the Father has sent Me, I also send you." And when He had said this, He breathed on them, and said to them, "Receive the Holy Spirit. If you forgive the sins of any, they are forgiven them; if you retain the sins of any, they are retained".

John 20:21-23

This was not a statement of intent but an impartation of the Holy Spirit to his followers. They actually received the Holy Spirit there and then. However, following this event they received a second experience of the Holy Spirit in power on the Day of Pentecost. The distinction is this; the Holy Spirit indwells the believer to seal their salvation but he empowers the believer for works of service.

The Acts of the Apostles contains further evidence that the Day of Pentecost was not the exception but the norm for believers. For example when Stephen preaches the gospel in Samaria, many genuine disciples are made with all the accompanying evidence. However, upon arrival of the apostles Peter and John from Jerusalem, Luke describes how these converts receive the Baptism of the Spirit.

> *Now when the apostles who were at Jerusalem heard that Samaria had received the word of God, they sent Peter and John to them, who, when they had come down, prayed for them that they might receive the Holy Spirit. For as yet He had fallen upon none of them. They had only been baptized in the name of the Lord Jesus. Then they laid hands on them, and they received the Holy Spirit.*
>
> Acts 8:14-17

A similar thing occurs in Acts chapter 19 when Paul meets some disciples in Ephesus. They had been baptized in John's baptism but not heard about the Holy Spirit. Paul filled in the blanks of their understanding and Luke describes what followed:

> *When they heard this, they were baptized in the name of the Lord Jesus. And when Paul had laid hands on them, the Holy Spirit came upon them,*

> *and they spoke with tongues and prophesied. Now the men were about twelve in all.*
>
> Acts 19:5-7

The Baptism with the Holy Spirit is our initiation into the realm of God's power. It is the point where we experience the anointing for the first time. Jesus had explained to the disciples, 'you shall receive power when the Holy Spirit has come upon you' (Acts 1:8). That is the anointing! The change experienced by the disciples on the Day of Pentecost was identical to my own the night I received the Baptism with the Holy Spirit. They were transformed into courageous champions of the gospel, preaching Christ and healing the sick. The church was born in the power of the Spirit and there is no evidence that God has wanted it any other way since.

Tongues and manifestations of the Spirit

The second thing I noticed in my Bible was that the Baptism with the Spirit was accompanied by 'speaking in tongues'. This is simply a language not previously known to the speaker but inspired by the Holy Spirit.

We see on the Day of Pentecost how the gathered disciples began exercising this gift as soon as the Holy Spirit had fallen on them in power. But this same phenomena is repeated elsewhere in the Book of Acts. When Peter preaches to a crowd of Gentiles in the home of the Roman Centurion Cornelius, Luke records:

> *While Peter was still speaking these words, the Holy Spirit fell upon all those who heard the word. And those of the circumcision who believed were astonished, as many as came with Peter, because the*

> *gift of the Holy Spirit had been poured out on the Gentiles also. For they heard them speak with tongues and magnify God.*
>
> Acts 10:44-46

Whenever the Holy Spirit was poured out in the Acts of the Apostles, the believers spoke in tongues, for example when Paul is with a group of disciples in the city of Ephesus he prays for them and the same thing occurs:

> *And when Paul had laid hands on them, the Holy Spirit came upon them, and they spoke with tongues and prophesied. Now the men were about twelve in all.*
>
> Acts 19:6-7

This new language inspired by the Holy Spirit is distinct from prayer and praise expressed in our normal language (Romans 8:26-27, 1 Corinthians 14:15). In 1 Corinthians 14:4 Paul states that 'he who speaks in a tongue builds himself up'. This kind of prayer inspired by the Holy Spirit is a powerful means for God to make us strong in our spirit.

Finally I observed that the Baptism with the Holy Spirit opens the believer up to a world of spiritual gifts or 'the manifestation of the Spirit' as Paul refers to it (1 Corinthians 12:7) including speaking in tongues. This is clearly explained by the apostle Paul in 1 Corinthians 12 where he describes nine such manifestations of the Holy Spirit's powerful presence. I have presented an overview of these nine gifts of the Spirit below by their category.

Category	Name	Description
Gifts of revelation	Word of wisdom	The supernatural ability to know what to do in a given situation
	Word of knowledge	Revelation knowledge about a person or situation given supernaturally
	Discerning of spirits	The supernatural ability to know the source by which someone speaks or acts
Gifts of declaration	Tongues	The supernatural ability to pray or prophesy in another language
	Interpretation of tongues	the ability to interpret the gift of tongues
	Prophecy	The supernatural ability to hear and speak the heart, mind and will of God
Gifts of demonstration	Faith	A sudden burst of faith above and beyond the level normally operated by the person operating this gift
	Gifts of healing	The supernatural ability to heal the sick
	Working of miracles	The supernatural ability to operate the miracle power of God

These gifts are the operation of the Holy Spirit through the life of the Spirit-baptized believer. The Holy Spirit inspires and directs their use as the occasion requires. By walking sensitively to the Holy Spirit we become aware of his promoting and step out in the use of them. In this way people are impacted by the presence and power of God; their needs are met, their lives are enriched and the kingdom of God is extended.

It's for today!

Even though the church was born in the power of the Spirit on the Day of Pentecost, much church history has been characterized by weakness and even denial of a distinct experience of the Holy Spirit after conversion. Despite this there have always been pockets of believers scattered through the world who experienced and practiced Pentecostal Christianity. There have also been powerful revival movements that were clearly the work of the Spirit though not necessarily carrying all the hallmarks of the Day of Pentecost.

The recovery of Pentecostal Christianity began toward the latter part of the 19th Century and the principal setting for this was the Holiness churches of North America. Mostly springing from a Methodist background, the Holiness movement put a value on seeking God for a deeper experience of the Holy Spirit. In addition to regular services with worship and preaching, they would hold 'tarrying meetings' where hungry believers were encouraged to wait on God. They were motivated by a desire for deeper sanctification, building on Methodist terminology of a 'second blessing' or experience of entire sanctification. But in time this evolved into full-blown Pentecostal language with the Baptism with the Spirit at its centre and a desire to experience the Spirit's power not just his purity.

Among many pioneers of this movement we should note Phoebe Palmer (1807-1874) who preached and taught extensively across the USA and Gt Britain as well as writing prolifically. She was a Methodist lay preacher who in 1840 began gathering people in her home for the pursuit of holiness.

Her influence grew until she was conducting revival meetings where thousands were converted. There is no doubt that on some of these occasions people were beginning to experience the Baptism with the Spirit and speaking in tongues.

Other influential Pentecostal pioneers at this time included A J Gordon (1836-1895), pastor of Clarendon Street Baptist Church in Boston Massachusetts. He taught clearly that the Baptism with the Holy Spirit was an experience distinct from new birth, characterized by spiritual power, speaking in tongues, healing and other spiritual gifts. We should also mention powerful evangelists like Charles Finney, D L Moody and R A Torrey who paved the way for Pentecostal Christianity. Between the years 1893 and 1900, twenty three new denominations formed within the Holiness movement in the USA, such was the growing hunger among believers for more of the Holy Spirit.

A major breakthrough came through the life and ministry of holiness preacher Charles Parham (1873-1929). He was hungry to know more of what was taking place among Holiness churches and this led him to visit the ministries of others who were seeking God for a deeper work of the Spirit. Finally he took the step of opening Bethel Bible College in Topeka, Kansas in the year 1900. From the time of its dedication in October of that year God began to work among the students culminating in a spontaneous move of the Spirit among the student body through the month of December.

In the watchnight service of December 31st 1900, the Holy Spirit manifest himself with unusual intensity. At 11.00pm one of the young students named Agnes Ozman, herself a holiness preacher, asked Parham to pray for her to receive the Baptism with the Spirit. Parham laid hands on her, prayed and immediately the glory of God fell on Agnes Ozman and she began speaking in fluent Chinese. Parham suspended normal activities and the college gave itself to a prolonged season of prayer. The flames of Pentecostal Christianity began to spread and Parham himself eventually received a mighty Holy Spirit Baptism.

The significance of Bethel Bible School was in providing a biblical link between a Pentecostal experience of the Baptism with the Holy Spirit and speaking in tongues as an accompanying sign. The pattern was set for what was to follow in the opening years of the 20th Century because the dam was soon about to break. Mighty moves of God continued to occur, most notably the Welsh Revival of 1904. The central instrument of God in this revival was a young man by the name of Evan Roberts. The Holy Spirit broke out in October 1904 at Moriah Chapel in the village of Loughor, South Wales and spread far and wide. It is reliably estimated that 100,000 souls came to Christ within a period of 18 months.

The 1904 Welsh revival was not so much characterized by Pentecostal manifestations but certainly contributed to the growing sense that God was at work in the world. It soon 'jumped' across the Atlantic and throughout 1905 pockets of revival were reported across the USA. The culmination to these events took place in Los Angeles in 1906 in what has become known as the Azousa Street revival. The heavens were opened and a full Pentecostal outpouring was ushered in and Charles Parham had a significant role in all this.

In 1905 Parham moved to Houston, Texas where he led a successful revival campaign and opened a short-term Bible School. One of those attracted to Parham and his school was a Black Holiness pastor named William Seymour. He enrolled onto the school where he learned all about the Baptism with the Holy Spirit. He had an intense hunger for God, devoting hours a day to prayer and seeking God for the fullness of the Holy Spirit. On completion of his studies Seymour responded to an invitation to pastor a Holiness congregation in Los Angeles and moved there in February 1906.

When he began however, the church officials rejected his emphasis on the Holy Spirit. However, Richard and Ruth Asberry who lived on Bonnie Bray Street, stepped in and invited Seymour to hold meetings in their home. It was here that the Holy Spirit began to move in power and word spread rapidly. A larger venue was needed and the meetings were moved to an empty building at 312 Azusa Street and the first service was held there on 14th April 1906. The fires of revival blazed even more brightly. The services were spontaneous and characterized by prayer. They would typically begin mid-morning and continue until well after midnight. The room itself was very simple with a pulpit made from shoe boxes. It is said that Seymour spent much of his time behind the pulpit in prayer, his head inside the top most shoe box!

News spread and soon thousands of people were passing through the meetings, curious to hear of the Spirit's activity and hungry to experience it for themselves. The Los Angeles Times gave local coverage and a Holiness journalist by the name of Frank Bartleman wrote many articles about the revival.

The flames of Pentecostal revival soon spread all over the United States and Canada. Ministers from overseas visited, received and carried the revival back with them to the nations of the world. The Azousa Street meetings themselves lasted only a few years before strife and division affected the original revival. But the move of God could not be stopped. Many ministries were raised up and countless Pentecostal churches formed in the following two decades.

Pentecostal Christianity continued to flourish in the 20th Century through successive fresh waves of renewal and blessing. This would include the Latter Rain Movement in the 1940's which originated in Canada and the USA Healing revivals of the 1950's. The Charismatic Movement of the 1960's and 70's came next with its origins in an obscure corner of, again, Los Angeles. A spiritually hungry Episcopalian minister by the name of Dennis Bennet experienced a baptism with the Holy Spirit on 3rd April 1960 at his church, St Marks, Van Nuys. It triggered spontaneous Charismatic experiences that soon spread far and wide. Dennis Bennet wrote about this in his landmark book 'Nine-O-Clock in the Morning' which became highly influential in stoking hunger in God's people all over the world.

The 1970's, 80's and 90's each saw their own distinctive contribution to Pentecostal and Charismatic Christianity which has developed to become the fastest growing branch of Christianity in the world. In many nations where there has been revival, believers have been initiated into the full Holy Spirit experience from the beginning and Holy Spirit churches and networks have sprung up everywhere.

Have you received?

Before we finish this chapter, I want to ensure that you have personally received your initial anointing – the Baptism with the Holy Spirit. I have observed how the Charismatic movement that was once such a force of God, has in some quarters become diluted and muddied. In the 1970's and 1980's people hungered for a personal experience of the Holy Spirit. Evangelical believers flocked to meetings where they might be prayed for to receive. Or they took time alone with God and prayed for the Holy Spirit. Then, not content with that, they sought God to speak in tongues. It mattered to them to receive everything God had in store for them.

Today sadly, this is not the case in many churches that outwardly have the appearance of being Charismatic. A personal experience of the Holy Spirit has been replaced with a worship style, service atmosphere and church culture that may look like the real thing but is often more about what happens on the stage than in the heart. Atmospheric lighting, smoke machines and 'sound pads' have become standard features in many churches. However, singing modern worship songs, raising your hands and feeling the atmosphere is not the same as a personal empowering encounter with the Holy Spirit. So how do you receive?

Sometimes believers receive the Baptism of the Holy Spirit purely at God's initiative. This is what happened to the Gentiles gathered in the home of Cornelius in Acts chapter 10. The Holy Spirit fell on the assembly as Peter was preaching. They must have believed what he said in their hearts by faith and God responded with an immediate Pentecostal outpouring. At other times the Baptism with the Holy Spirit is given in answer to the prayer of hunger from the heart of the seeker. I know of many people who in the privacy of their home simply asked God to fill them and he did.

Finally, the Baptism with the Spirit can be received through the laying on of hands, as in Samaria with Peter and John or in Ephesus with Paul. 'When Paul placed his hands on them, the Holy Spirit came on them and they spoke in tongues and prophesied' (Acts 19:5). A servant of God will place their hands on the head of the seeker and pray a prayer of faith for them to receive. This was my experience when I received the Holy Spirit. Looking at it from the seeker's point of view however, we receive Holy Spirit baptism in the same way as we receive all the blessing of God – by faith.

First, you need to ask the Lord to cleanse you from all outstanding sin so that you can approach him with confidence. In other words, you need to clear your conscience (Acts 24:16). Create a clear landing strip for the Holy Spirit.

Then it is important to actually ask your heavenly Father for the gift of Holy Spirit. Jesus said, 'If you . . . though you are evil, know how to give good gifts to your children, how much more will your Father in heaven give the Holy Spirit to those who ask him' (Luke 11:13).

Having prayed, and believing God has heard your prayer, begin to praise God and worship him with thanksgiving. This is a powerful way of drawing near to his presence to receive the Holy Spirit. In his letter James says, 'Draw near to God and he will draw near to you' (James 4:8). Expect to receive from God. No one in the Bible was ever baptized with the Holy Spirit and didn't know it. If this is taking place in a public meeting you may have responded to an altar call for ministry and a servant of God may lay hands on you to impart the Holy Spirit.

Finally, open your mouth and begin to speak in tongues. God will not force himself upon you. He requires our cooperation, so begin to form syllables and keep the focus of your attention on worshipping Jesus and the language will flow. If you feel you are stuck, there is nothing wrong in visiting a church you know that has an emphasis on the full Pentecostal experience. Ask for prayer. Seek out someone to lay hands on you for the Baptism with the Spirit. God is faithful. He wants every one of his children to enjoy their full inheritance of Spirit filled Christianity.

2

What is the anointing?

Our English word 'anointing' originates from the Old Testament Hebrew word *massiah.* Sometimes it is not translated and simply appears as the title 'messiah'. The New Testament word for anointing is *christos.* This is where the title 'Christ' comes from. The Christ is the anointed one or messiah sent by God to deliver his people from their enemies.

It is important to understand that the word 'Christ' was not Jesus' surname or family name. He was more accurately described as Jesus of Nazareth. The word 'Christ' was his title, a recognition that he was the anticipated messiah. When the man Jesus of Nazareth was anointed with the Holy Spirit he became the Christ of God.

If we really want to understand the purpose of the anointing today we have to appreciate the central role that Jesus the Son of God has in history as the great anointed one of God, the messiah. In order to do that we need to start at the beginning and discover where all the pieces fit together that lead us up to the appearance of Christ, the anointed one, himself.

God's original purpose

God created Adam to be the pinnacle of creation, the closest thing to God himself, made in his very image and likeness. He was created to have dominion over creation, to walk in intimacy with his heavenly father and alongside Eve, to populate the earth with God's family. David speaks of it in this way:

> *What is man, that thou art mindful of him? And the son of man, that thou visitest him? For thou hast made him but little lower than God, And crownest him with glory and honor. Thou makest him to have dominion over the works of thy hands; Thou hast put all things under his feet.*
>
> Psalms 8:4-6 ASV

When God created Adam he didn't just make a superior creature, he brought a son into the world. We see that from Luke 3:28 where Luke refers to, 'Adam, the son of God'. God purposed to have an earthly family and he gave Adam and Eve the task of producing that family for him. Everything went well until Eve, and then Adam with her, both fell into temptation at the hands of God's sworn enemy, Satan.

When Adam sinned it was catastrophic. We call this 'the fall'. Adam fell from his lofty position, sin entered the world and mankind was separated from God. But the effects of Adam's disobedience were much greater. In that moment he transferred his allegiance from God his heavenly Father to Satan. In doing so he handed a degree of authority over to Satan. As a consequence humanity came under a terrible sentence of death. Sin entered the world and with it all the brokenness we see around us today.

But more than that, when Adam sinned he became a spiritual orphan – he was separated from his heavenly Father and became allied with Satan. Orphan-heartedness describes exactly, the condition of men and women today. Just as the younger son walked out of the father's house in the story of the prodigal, we are separated and isolated from the God who made us and loves us.

But even in the moment of catastrophe and failure, God swooped in and secured his continued purpose. He didn't destroy his creation. He didn't consign Adam and Eve to the dustbin of history. Instead God did a remarkable thing. He introduced a plan of redemption.

> *So the LORD God said to the serpent: "Because you have done this, you are cursed more than all cattle, and more than every beast of the field; on your belly you shall go, and you shall eat dust all the days of your life. And I will put enmity between you and the woman, and between your seed and her Seed; He shall bruise your head, and you shall bruise His heel."*
>
> Genesis 3:14-15

The prophetic word contained in this passage reveals God's plan of salvation for mankind for he promises a deliverer – a messiah – one born of the human race who would rescue mankind from Satan's oppression. Satan would bruise messiah's heel but messiah would crush Satan's head! This statement indicated that victory over Satan would come at a cost. The messiah would himself suffer, but win a decisive victory over Satan. With those words, the fate of the devil was sealed. Adam and Eve knew it and I believe, lived in the good of it, aware that their failure was not the end of the story. A deliverer would arise from their own offspring.

Although they had attempted to cover their shame with home-made clothes, God himself came to their aid. He slew animals, skinned them and provided a covering for their sin. This was of course a powerful sign of how the ultimate victory over sin would be won. Another living creature gave its life for Adam and Eve. Their sin and shame were covered through sacrifice. More than that, Adam and Eve accepted this covering from God's merciful hand and in so doing, the way was opened for man to continue in a new basis of relationship with God.

Now Satan was forced to listen to the prophetic word spoken against him but inwardly fought the sentence of death. From then on he would be on the lookout for anyone who might fit the profile of the saviour. Down through the ages he kept vigilant watch in order to identify and snuff out any threat to himself. On the flip side of this, the Old Testament people of Israel lived in the expectation of their messiah, who would rescue them from their enemies and establish the kingdom of God on the earth. And as you read the Old Testament you can recognise such characters popping up from its pages. We are going to look at two of them later from the Book of Judges. But there are other examples;

- Moses – led the people of Israel out of Egypt and through the wilderness
- David – delivered the people from the Philistine and established God's kingdom
- Esther – interceded with King Ahasuerus for the people of Israel

All of these were types or shadows of the Christ who was to come. God raised them up to deliver his people at crucial moments of history. There are other aspects to the Old Covenant ministry of the messiah that I cover in the appendix to this book, for those who are interested in exploring more.

The Christ appears

Finally, after many hundreds of years, the hope and expectation of God's Old Testament people was fulfilled in the birth of

Jesus of Nazareth. Notice how the angel announced his birth to the shepherds:

> *Then the angel said to them, "Do not be afraid, for behold, I bring you good tidings of great joy which will be to all people. For there is born to you this day in the city of David* ***a Savior, who is Christ the Lord.****"*
>
> Luke 2:10-12

The long awaited messiah had arrived in the person of Jesus. He then grew under the guidance of his parents, lived an obscure life until the age of 30, at which point he entered his life's work. Luke describes Jesus' anointed ministry in the Book of Acts in this way:

> *. . . how* ***God anointed Jesus of Nazareth*** *with the Holy Spirit and with power, who went about doing good and healing all who were oppressed by the devil, for God was with Him.*
>
> Acts 10:38

But when exactly was Jesus anointed with the Holy Spirit? It was not at his birth. He was conceived and born as the Son of God but his anointed ministry did not begin until he was an adult. Until then he was hidden from view and lived in obscurity. The devil did not know who Jesus of Nazareth was! He performed no miracle, cast out no demons and healed no sick bodies. He was veiled from Satan's sight until the precise moment.

All that changed when one day at the age of 30 he walked down to the Jordan River and met John the Baptist. It was here, when he was baptized by John at the Jordan that Jesus was anointed with the Holy Spirit. As he came out of the water the Holy Spirit descended upon him like a dove and he was launched into his supernatural ministry of miracles, healing and deliverance. Jesus of Nazareth became the Christ of God. This is how Luke describes the events on that day.

> *When all the people were baptized, it came to pass that Jesus also was baptized; and while He prayed, the heaven was opened. And the Holy Spirit descended in bodily form like a dove upon Him, and a voice came from heaven which said, "You are My beloved Son; in You I am well pleased."*
>
> Luke 3:21-22

Here is the order of events:

- *'The heaven was opened'* – A new level of communication was established between heaven and earth centred in the Son of God.
- *'The Holy Spirit descended in bodily form like a dove upon Him'* – At that moment Jesus of Nazareth became the anointed Christ of God.
- *'A voice came from heaven which said, "You are my beloved Son; in you I am well pleased."'* The father took the wraps off his Son and announced him to the powers of darkness and to the world.

You can see the way Jesus was recognised as the Christ when Andrew, one of the disciples, came to his brother Simon Peter with an announcement. '"We have found the Messiah" (which is translated, the Christ). And he brought him to Jesus' (John 1:41-42). Similarly the woman of Samaria knew what to expect in the messiah. She said to Jesus, 'I know that Messiah is coming (who is called Christ). When He comes, He will tell us all things' (John 4:25).

Although the Old Testament people of God were looking for their messiah, Jesus did not meet their expectations and that is why they largely rejected him. They were hoping for political and military deliverance from their Roman oppressors. Jesus came with a revolutionary shift in their understanding of the kingdom of God and salvation. It would be firstly internal and spiritual, working in the hearts of men and women. Then it would develop into righteous living. Next it would manifest in the church community and finally in society itself. God has not abandoned the Jews however, and a great harvest is approaching when they will realise that Jesus is their messiah and turn to him in large numbers.

Definitions

What is the anointing? What does the word mean? To anoint means to rub, smear or cover, especially with reference to oil or fat. Unlike water, oil will not evaporate, it lingers and there is a clue to the significance of the anointing, it speaks of permanence. Our English word 'ointment' is a direct translation of the word 'anointing' and of course describes this point exactly; ointment is a medicinal cream that is rubbed into the skin. During anointing ceremonies oil is poured over the head of the one being appointed to a particular office or recognized by God to fulfil a divine purpose. Here is how the prophet Samuel anointed David who at this time was a simple shepherd boy:

> *And the LORD said, "Arise, anoint him; for this is the one!" Then Samuel took the horn of oil and anointed him in the midst of his brothers; and the Spirit of the LORD came upon David from that day forward. So Samuel arose and went to Ramah.*
>
> 1 Samuel 16:12-13

Do you notice what the Scripture verse says here? David was anointed, 'from that day forward'. Once anointed, God is reluctant to remove his blessing from the life of a man or woman because, as we shall see, the anointing is the power to fulfil a commission to a task. So what is the anointing? I have a simple definition based on the Hebrew and Greek words and how they are used in the Bible.

> *"The anointing of the Holy Spirit is the* ***presence*** *of the Holy Spirit on a* ***person*** *with* ***power*** *to fulfil the* ***purpose*** *of God on the earth."*

When these four elements are combined together they form the spiritual chemistry of the anointing:

- *The presence* – the anointing is the manifestation of God the Holy Spirit himself
- *On a person* – the anointing always sits or rests on the life of a human being
- *In power* – the anointing is the supernatural power of God
- *For a purpose* – the anointing is always given for a reason

Let's break this down further.

- **Presence**

The anointing is more than the influence, evidence or even the power that the Spirit of God gives. It is God himself. The Holy Spirit is the third person of the trinity. This is the incredible truth we will keep returning to. Time after time we read expressions like these in the life of Samson;

And the Spirit of the LORD came mightily upon him, and he tore the lion apart as one would have torn apart a young goat, though he had nothing in his hand.

Judges 14:6

Then the Spirit of the LORD came upon him mightily, and he went down to Ashkelon and killed thirty of their men, took their apparel, and gave the changes of clothing to those who had explained the riddle.

Judges 14:19

When he came to Lehi, the Philistines came shouting against him. Then the Spirit of the LORD came mightily upon him; and the ropes that were on his arms became like flax that is burned with fire, and his bonds broke loose from his hands.

Judges 15:14

The presence of God may be gentle or it may be violent. It may come with physical manifestation or not. However, regardless of appearances, the anointing is always the very presence of God himself. Jesus said, '. . . when He, the Spirit of truth, has come, He will guide you into all truth . . .' (John 16:13). The Holy Spirit is a person! His anointing is his presence in power and you are conscious of him.

- **Person**

The anointing of the Holy Spirit can only and always rest on a human being. The anointing always connects God and man together. God seeks for people he can land on. He is always on the lookout for suitable human landing strips for a heavenly visitation. This is what he found on the Day of Pentecost, the best divine runway possible, in the form of 120 spiritually hungry men and women.

The anointing should not be treated lightly or casually but with a holy fear and reverence. It is the person of the Holy Spirit resting on mortal and imperfect human beings. Samson ultimately lost his anointing because he despised his Nazarite calling. When Samson divulged the secret of his strength and his hair was shorn, the Book of Judges records the tragic result in this way:

> *So he awoke from his sleep, and said, "I will go out as before, at other times, and shake myself free!" But he did not know that the LORD had departed from him.*
>
> Judges 16:20

It wasn't simply the power or strength of the Spirit that he lost, but the Lord himself had departed from him. The presence of God withdrew from a person.

- **Power**

The presence of the Holy Spirit can be felt and experienced in many ways; his peace, his love, his still small voice and his comfort, for example. All of these are wonderful but the anointing is different – it is the power of the Holy Spirit. The word used time and again in the New Testament to describe this anointing power is the Greek word *dunamis*. From this word we derive English words like 'dynamo', 'dynamic' and 'dynamite'! That should serve as a clue to its meaning! Before his departure from the earth Jesus spoke these words to his disciples;

> *. . . you shall receive **power** (dunamis) when the Holy Spirit has come upon you; and you shall be witnesses to Me in Jerusalem, and in all Judea and Samaria, and to the end of the earth.*
>
> Acts 1:8

This power resulted in direct divine ability to do what could not be done by even the best of human strength or endevours. No wonder Jesus told his disciples to wait in Jerusalem until they had received it. He wanted their success to be assured and guaranteed. This power accompanied them through the course of the Book of Acts. When they faced fresh challenges, such as threats of persecution as in Acts chapter 4, they simply received more of the same! God showed up when they prayed; the place where they met was shaken and they were all filled again!

- **Purpose**

The anointing represents the purpose-aspect of the Holy Spirit's presence. Every one of us is anointed for a purpose to do the works of God and fulfil the reason God gave us life and breath. His anointing takes a multitude of forms. We are not all called to be preachers or pastors and it is vital to recognise that there is no spiritual-secular divide when it comes to the call and gifting of God. You may be anointed to the field of business, or medicine, or government, or the arts. You may be called to occupy a factory floor or a boardroom, to drive a taxi or an airplane. There is no calling too humble for God to anoint. There is no occupation too lofty in the world's eyes to exempt you from the anointing.

Brother Lawrence was a 17th Century French war veteran. Wounded in conflict he became a monk and worked the rest of his life in the kitchen of a monastery near Paris. Yet so profound was the anointing of God on his life that a record of some of his conversations and letters, captured and recorded, has remained a literary classic for 300 years. He carried such a sweetness of God's presence that visitors became aware of this as soon as they were in his company. People would travel for miles just to sit and talk with him.

There is an anointing to receive inventions and design products. There is an anointing to counsel, comfort and advice. There is an anointing to create and distribute wealth. There is an anointing to do business. God wills that everything in life can be conducted in the power that the Spirit gives; raising children, managing finances, purchasing a house, cooking, gardening, working and resting.

There is a foundational level to the anointing. We saw this in the previous chapter; it is called the Baptism with the Holy Spirit. It is frequently accompanied by speaking in tongues, prophecy and other spiritual gifts. These are things which are given to 'those who believe' (Mark 16:17) not just the specialists. Then there is the broader range of spiritual gifts that Paul outlines in 1 Corinthians 12 like the word of wisdom, miracles and healing.

Finally God invites us in to live an anointed life where every conscious moment is lived for him and infused by his Spirit; where every word and every activity is permeated with his presence. This is God's goal. Life is lived for Christ in abundance and everything contributes to God's purpose to win the lost, build his church and establish his kingdom in the earth.

Two important Questions

With this understanding of what the anointing really is, I trust you are feeling more qualified than before and hungrier than ever to receive and operate in the anointing. If so, if you are seeking God for a greater anointing, there are two important questions you should be asking yourself.

- What task has God anointed you for?

Many believers ask God for more; more of his Spirit, more of his power, more of his presence. My question is, 'what do you want that anointing for?' The anointing is never an end in itself. It is always, absolutely always, given for a reason. We are anointed for something. What is the something God has called you to do for which you need the anointing?

Later on I refer to the story of Samson to teach us some lessons on the anointing. Whenever the Spirit of God came on Samson in power it was always to accomplish a task before him. He was anointed to get a job done and he knew what that job was. This also holds true for all the deliverers we read of in the Book of Judges. God called them to do something and anointed them for the task.

Of course, we want Jesus for his own sake. We do not ever need to justify why we want more of him. He is an end in himself. Everything we do is all about Jesus. But when we ask for more of the anointing that is something different. The anointing is given to fulfil God's purpose on the earth. So what are you seeking that anointing for?

- What are you doing with the anointing you have already received?

The second question leads on from the first. If you are seeking more anointing, what are you doing with what God has already given you? If you have experienced the Holy Spirit in power to any discernable degree, then it was given you for a purpose. Are you pursuing that purpose?

You may be genuinely unclear about this. Perhaps you have been part of a church environment where the Holy Spirit was always and only spoken about in terms of your needs and feelings. Perhaps the anointing was not spoken of at all.

Whatever the cause, without doubt, once you begin to move in the known will of God, you will soon discover the joy and privilege of His presence in power with you.

There is a simple principle in the kingdom of God. If you are faithful with little you will be entrusted with more (Luke 16:10). If you are pursuing God's purpose for your life, enlisting the gifts and opportunities he has given to you, then you are already in prime position for an anointing upgrade. God has no problem getting more power to your life. You do not need to chase the anointing as if it was trying to evade you. God is after you and he knows how to hit a moving target!

I own a mechanical automatic watch. It needs no battery to power it because the watch movement converts the energy from the motion of my hand and winds up the spring with it. Then the energy stored in the spring powers the mechanism of the watch. When I bought it I noticed that every few days it made a strange whirring noise unlike other mechanical watches I have owned. I took it back to the shop from which I bought it and one of the engineers explained that this is what they call an energy dump.

You see, my physical movements were storing up so much energy, the spring was fully wound and could receive no more. So the watch had a way of releasing that energy so as not to overwind the spring. That was the noise and vibration I was sensing. When this was being explained I heard the Lord say that this is what is often happening in his people. They ask for more but there is nowhere for it to go because there is insufficient movement to keep pace with the input of his energy and power!

Jesus is the model and marker for the anointing. He was a man empowered by the Holy Spirit. He fulfilled his supernatural ministry not as the Son of God but as a man in relationship with his father and anointed with the Holy Spirit.

In doing this he paved the way for you and me to live and minister in exactly the same way. Jesus stripped himself of his advantage in order to show us what a Spirit filled, Spirit anointed man walking in intimacy with the Father looks like.

Christ in his ministry

Let's go back to the events of Jesus' baptism and what took place next. Before his anointing at the Jordan Jesus performed no miracle, healed no sick person, cast out no demon spirit. His identity was kept under wraps by the Father. The devil did not know that the Carpenter's son from Nazareth was the seed of the woman who would spell his downfall.

As we saw in the previous chapter all that changed the day Jesus stepped out of the Carpenter's shop and made his way to the Jordon River to be baptized by John the Baptist. John knew who he was of course and protested as to why he should be baptizing the Christ. But Jesus proceeded as planned, waded into the water and was baptized by John. At that moment everything changed. The instant the Son of God was revealed to the world Satan saw his opportunity and pounced. Five thousand years of watching and waiting and here he is. The seed of the woman has arrived and the devil made his move.

Jesus was led by the Spirit into the desert to be tempted by the devil and Satan threw everything he could at the Son of God. For forty days and nights he faced the full onslaught of God's sworn enemy alone. He overcame every temptation thrown at him through his surrender to the father and his Father's will. He was now ready to begin the mission for which he had been sent. Luke records how these events unfolded:

> *Then Jesus returned in the power of the Spirit to Galilee, and news of Him went out through all*

> *the surrounding region. And He taught in their synagogues, being glorified by all. So He came to Nazareth, where He had been brought up. And as His custom was, He went into the synagogue on the Sabbath day, and stood up to read. And He was handed the book of the prophet Isaiah. And when He had opened the book, He found the place where it was written: "The Spirit of the LORD is upon Me, Because He has anointed Me To preach the gospel to the poor; He has sent Me to heal the brokenhearted, To proclaim liberty to the captives And recovery of sight to the blind, To set at liberty those who are oppressed; To proclaim the acceptable year of the LORD." Then He closed the book, and gave it back to the attendant and sat down. And the eyes of all who were in the synagogue were fixed on Him. And He began to say to them, "Today this Scripture is fulfilled in your hearing."*
>
> Luke 4:14-21

Jesus went into the desert in the power of the Spirit; he came out of the desert in the power of the Spirit. He began travelling the Galilee area, teaching, preaching and healing the sick. Then he deliberately made his way to the synagogue in Nazareth, opened the scroll of the prophet Isaiah and read the passage we know as chapter 61.

In reading this passage from Isaiah Jesus was announcing his messianic mission. He declared the purpose for which the Holy Spirit had anointed him. 'The Spirit of the Lord is upon me because he has anointed me to . . .' Everything we have observed about the anointing was present here in Jesus; the **presence** of the Spirit upon a **person** (Jesus) in **power** to fulfil God's **purpose**.

On that day in Nazareth, Jesus announced the ministry for which he had come. He presented his ministry mandates. These are a prescription of what he did for three and one half years among the Jewish people. If we sit Luke 4:18-19 alongside Isaiah 61:1-2 we get the best picture of these mandates:

- *'Good news for the poor'* – this refers to forgiveness of sins which sets us free from guilt and shame. We were condemned until Jesus paid the price and set us free.
- *'Healing of the broken hearted'* – Jesus came to restore us from all the destruction that sin has produced in individuals, families and society. He came to heal all who have been emotionally and mentally damaged and scarred.
- *'Recovery of sight to the blind'* – this is a motif for physical healing of every kind. Healing is absolutely central to the gospel. Jesus healed the sick. The disciples healed the sick and healing remains on God's agenda for today.
- *'Liberty to the captives'* – this refers to Jesus' ministry of casting out evil spirits. Demonic activity is real and Jesus gave us authority over evil spirits and every form of demonic oppression.

We are going to look at this in greater depth but for now it is vital we note that everything God is doing in the earth today finds its roots somewhere in these mandates because the mission of Christ has not changed. What he began, the church continues until Jesus returns. You and I are part of that great purpose and that is why God has an anointing for you!

3

The promise of the father

In November 1945 my father arrived back home from his time serving in the army during the Second World War. He was active throughout that war. He was one of the 340,000 soldiers rescued from the beaches of Dunkirk on 26th May 1940. He was then posted to the Far East and was among thousands of Allied servicemen captured by the Japanese in Singapore in January 1942. He was marched north over many days and put to forced labour building the infamous Thai-Burmese railway. Thousands of men did not survive this brutal experience, including an uncle I never met.

In the summer of 1944 my father was taken across the South China Sea to Japan in one of the infamous 'death ships'. These were basically cargo ships that the Japanese used to ferry their slave labour in the most appalling conditions. In Japan he worked at a Zinc foundry in Nagasaki. Walking back to the prison camp on the 6th August 1945, the sky was lit up by the atomic bomb that was dropped on the city of Nagasaki. The war in the Far East was over.

The newly liberated prisoners of war were in a terrible condition. Hospital treatment and a long journey home awaited my father. It took him 3 months before he arrived back in England, via Manila in the Philippines, across the Pacific Ocean stopping at Hawaii, and then on to San Francisco. This was followed by a three day train journey across the USA to New York. His voyage across the Atlantic to Southampton took place aboard the Ocean liner the Queen Mary. Finally two train journeys and a short walk and he arrived in Westcliff on Sea in Essex and to his homecoming welcome.

The homecoming I have described would have been replicated tens of thousands of times across the UK as servicemen were reunited with their families and loved ones. There was victory to celebrate, medals to display, stories to tell. Some would have been quiet and private affairs, others would have been noisy gatherings of family and friends. But none of those celebrations compared to the greatest homecoming of all time – the victorious return of Jesus the Son of God to his Father in heaven!

I want you to imagine with me, what that Ascension Day must have looked like! Think about it. Here comes Jesus, victorious over sin, risen from the dead and walking majestically and joyfully through the courts of heaven as he approaches the throne of God. He is returning to the place from which he was sent. But this time – mystery of mysteries, wonder of wonders – he is clothed in a resurrected human body. That body bore the scars of his suffering and death. In the Book of Revelation John speaks of a lamb standing before the throne of God, 'as if it had just been slain' (Revelation 5:6). Jesus returns to heaven bearing the form of his humanity.

A multitude of angels stand in line, waiting to welcome him and proclaim his return to heaven. Psalm 24:7-10 speaks prophetically of the moment in this way, as a herald angel cries out to the assembly:

> *'Lift up your heads, O you gates! And be lifted up, you everlasting doors! And the King of glory shall come in.'*

A second angel asks the question,

> *'Who is this King of glory?'*

The first angel replies,

> *'The LORD strong and mighty, The LORD mighty in battle. Lift up your heads, O you gates! Lift up, you everlasting doors! And the King of glory shall come in.'*

The second angel repeats his question,

> *'Who is this King of glory?'*

Once again the first angel cries out,

> *'The LORD of hosts, He is the King of glory.'*

The Son draws right up to the throne of God; the Father receives him and offers him a place next to him. David describes the moment in Psalm 110, 'The LORD said to my Lord, "Sit at my right hand, till I make your enemies your footstool"' (Psalms 110:1). The Son speaks to the Father; 'I have fulfilled everything that was required of me. Now it is time for me to receive the promise'. Wait a minute, is that correct? Did Jesus actually claim a promise from the Father? If so, what was that promise and how did it come about? We are going to find out because what happened next would change the spiritual landscape of the world in a moment. What exactly is the promise of the Father?

The Promise Given

As Jesus approached the time for him to return to his Father he prepared the disciples with these words;

> *Behold, I send the Promise of My Father upon you; but tarry in the city of Jerusalem until you are endued with power from on high.*
>
> Luke 24:49

So Jesus speaks of 'the promise of the Father' to the disciples but where does this expression originate? Why is it so important that it was referred to by Jesus and later on by Peter? To answer these questions we need to go to the Old Testament and specifically the book of the prophecy of Joel:

> *And it shall come to pass afterward That I will pour out my Spirit on all flesh; Your sons and your daughters shall prophesy, Your old men shall dream dreams, Your young men shall see visions. And also on my menservants and on my maidservants I will pour out my Spirit in those days. "And I will show wonders in the heavens and in the earth: Blood and fire and pillars of smoke. The sun shall be turned into darkness, and the moon into blood, before the coming of the great and awesome day of the LORD. And it shall come to pass that whoever calls on the name of the LORD shall be saved. For in Mount Zion and in Jerusalem there shall be deliverance, As the LORD has said, among the remnant whom the LORD calls.*
>
> Joel 2:28-32

Bible commentators are divided when it comes to putting a date on the prophecy of Joel. They are either of the view that Joel was one of the very earliest prophets or that he was one of the last. I sit in the second camp. I believe Joel lived and prophesied around 350 BC for a simple reason. God unfolds his purposes through the Old Testament prophets in a progressive journey of revelation.

As we approach the latter prophets like Jeremiah or Ezekiel, and we see the failure of God's people Israel, more and more amazing revelation is unveiled concerning what God is going to do in the future. The prophets announce the coming of a New Covenant – very different to the Covenant of Moses which the people failed to keep. This New Covenant would be characterized by an internal change of heart rather than an external demand of the law. This would be made possible by the power of the Holy Spirit being given to all who would receive God's offer of salvation by faith.

Joel's prophecy of the outpouring of the Holy Spirit fits directly in line with this unfolding revelation. It represents a climax of prophecy. He describes the giving of the Holy Spirit on this New Covenant people. More than that, the prophecy of Joel contains a solemn commitment on the part of God to make the Holy Spirit available to all God's people.

In Joel chapter 2 God the Father makes a promise that the day would come when he would pour out his Holy Spirit on all flesh. No longer would this be confined to the special offices of prophet, priest and king. A new dispensation and administration of the Spirit would be enjoyed by all through the introduction of a New Covenant. God would pour out His Spirit on 'all flesh'.

This New Covenant would be secured in and through the blood of God's own Son Jesus. It would be a covenant of the Spirit. No longer would the commands of God stand against the people of God as a statement of their failure, Instead, they would be written on the inside, on the heart, and the Holy Spirit would be the power to keep the commands. This is the promise of the Father!

But how do we know for sure that Joel's prophecy is the promise of the Father referred to by Jesus in Luke 24:49? We simply have to go to the Book of Acts and see for ourselves what both Jesus and Peter said about this. First of all here is Jesus describing the promise:

> *And being assembled together with them, He commanded them not to depart from Jerusalem, but to wait for* ***the Promise of the Father****, "which," He said, "you have heard from me; for John truly baptized with water, but you shall be baptized with the Holy Spirit not many days from now."*
>
> Acts 1:4-5

So Jesus is identifying the promise of the Father as the outpouring of the Spirit that was to take place on the Day of Pentecost. Now look a little further into chapter 2 after the Holy Spirit had fallen on the disciples and notice how Peter interprets what had occurred when he addresses the gathered crowd on the Day of Pentecost:

> *This Jesus God has raised up, of which we are all witnesses. Therefore being exalted to the right hand of God, and* ***having received from the Father the promise of the Holy Spirit****, He poured out this which you now see and hear.*
>
> Acts 2:32-33

So Peter says the same thing as Jesus; the promise of the Father is the outpouring of the Holy Spirit, the anointing that God gave the disciples on the Day of Pentecost.

The promise to who?

The next question we need to answer is, to whom was God the Father making the promise? It would be easy to assume that the promise had been made to the disciples or the early church. In this case God the father would be promising his people that he would pour out his Spirit upon them. This would be entirely reasonable but it is not the case. The fact is the promise of the Father was made to Jesus the Son! Peter says, 'having received from the father, the promised Holy Spirit he has poured out . . .' (Acts 2:33). Yes, in the far reaches of eternity, between the persons of the Godhead, the Father had made a promise to the Son. In doing so the Father and the Son had joined themselves in a solemn covenant for the rescue of mankind.

Some theologians refer to this as the covenant of redemption. It was a promise from the Father that if Jesus the Son of God was willing to strip himself of his eternal glory, come to earth and be born in human flesh, carry the love of God to mortal men and women, represent him in life, die an agonizing death on the cross for the sins of the world – then the Father would raise him up from the dead, exalt him to his right hand once more, rescue men and women from their sins and pour out the Holy Spirit on all who owned the name of Jesus.

God's majestic plan of redemption for mankind was dependent on this binding agreement between the persons of the Trinity – and not just the Father and the Son, but the Holy Spirit too, as he would be the one to visit the earth in grace and power and inhabit God's blood bought children. What an incredible plan. What an awesome God we serve!

So Jesus the Son and the Holy Spirit agreed with the Father and a covenant of love was made that committed the Godhead to this master plan. In the fullness of time Jesus stripped himself of his glory, came to live among us as a man, suffered for the sins of the world and died a terrible death on the cross. In turn God the father raised Jesus from the dead on the third day, just as he had promised, with an incorruptible, resurrection body. In this form Jesus spent 40 days among his disciples, teaching them about the kingdom of God and preparing them for their future mission before his ascension back to heaven.

Now let's pick the story back up as Jesus ascends to heaven and approaches the throne of God. I am going to use some sanctified imagination here. The Father acknowledges the Son, 'Well done my Son. The Holy Spirit is ready and waiting'. The Father and the Son turn to the Holy Spirit and just as at creation, the Spirit is himself ready, hovering, waiting. Father and Son say 'Go!'

At exactly the same time at a location in Jerusalem, the 120 disciples of Jesus are gathered, waiting and praying. Nothing could have prepared them for what was about to happen. They are following Jesus' instruction to wait in Jerusalem until they are clothed with power. But they have no idea what that is going to look like. The moment the Holy Spirit is sent from heaven, he descends like lightening on the gathered company, baptizes them in his power and love and the rest as they say, is history.

Heaven on earth

So why is the promise of the Father so important? Why did Jesus and Peter refer to it so specifically? The answer is simple. It demonstrates with absolute certainty that God did not abandon the earth when his Son returned to heaven! Rather, the three persons of the Trinity had bound themselves in a solemn commitment to redeem a people and empower them with the same anointing that was on the Son to do the same works that the Son did during his earthly ministry. The outpouring of the Holy Spirit is the literal proof that Jesus has risen from the dead, that he sits on the throne of heaven and that the future of the world is secure.

The implications of this are enormous. Whatever we see going on around us; whatever the state of the world; whatever chaos and conflict may take place – underneath it all the world is being preserved by a covenant between the persons of the Trinity. While the church fulfils her ministry God is protecting her and providing for everything she needs. This means the church is literally the continuation of the Christ, his body on the earth. We are the baton-carriers of the purpose of God that Jesus instigated during his own life and ministry.

This is the message of this book. God invaded the world in the person of his Son, and anointed him with the Holy Spirit. When Jesus left the planet he handed his ministry on to his disciples to continue in the power of the Spirit. That is the way it is until Christ returns! Luke begins the book of Acts in this way:

> *The former account I made, O Theophilus, of all that Jesus began both to do and teach, until the day in which He was taken up, after He through the Holy Spirit had given commandments to the apostles whom He had chosen.*
>
> Acts 1:1-2

So the gospels are the record of what Jesus *began* to do and to teach. The Acts of the Apostles is the record of what he *continues* to do and to teach – except that now it is through his church, the many membered body of Christ. That purpose continues uninterrupted through the centuries to this day. Sometimes the fire of the Holy Spirit has burned hot and strong. At other times the fire of God's power has just smoldered in the church. But through the ages God has been restoring, establishing and reviving his people and his purpose.

Today approaching 2 billion people own the name of Jesus. But perhaps more significantly than that, Pentecostal/ Charismatic believers are the fastest growing expression of the church in the world today. We are going to unwrap the mind-blowing implication of a Spirit-filled church soon. But let me give you a little fore-taste. It is time for the church to raise her expectation, for every child of God to step up to the plate and claim the full inheritance of the Holy Spirit and His power that the Father has promised.

> *Christ has redeemed us from the curse of the law, having become a curse for us (for it is written, "Cursed is everyone who hangs on a tree"), that the blessing of Abraham might come upon the Gentiles in Christ Jesus,* ***that we might receive the promise of the Spirit through faith.***
>
> Galatians 3:13-14

Jesus suffered and shed his blood for us to be forgiven of all our sin. But that is only half the equation. Our salvation is provided so we can become vessels of God's power. We receive the promise of the Holy Spirit just as Jesus did to do the works of God just as Jesus did.

The church – the extension of Christ

Before his ascension, Jesus was one man anointed by the Holy Spirit. From the Day of Pentecost, a multiplication took place. The Holy Spirit was transferred from Jesus to 120 disciples. The body of Christ became a many membered Spirit-anointed body. Then on that first day the 120 became 3,000 when the people responded to Peter's message. This number soon swelled to multiple thousands until this new 'sect' known as Christians could be found throughout the Roman Empire. Jesus was no longer confined to a physical body but present by his Spirit through the church, every member indwelt by and filled with the same Holy Spirit that had rested on Jesus.

The Day of Pentecost was the occasion God anointed the disciples with the Spirit. Here is what Luke says:

> *When the Day of Pentecost had fully come, they were all with one accord in one place. And suddenly there came a sound from heaven, as of a rushing mighty wind, and it filled the whole house where they were sitting. Then there appeared to them divided tongues, as of fire, and one sat upon each of them. And they were all filled with the Holy Spirit and began to speak with other tongues, as the Spirit gave them utterance.*
>
> Acts 2:1-4

The church is the body of Christ on earth and Jesus is the head of the body in heaven. Paul explains this in some of his letters particularly to the Ephesians, Colossians and Corinthians.

> *. . . He raised Him from the dead and seated Him at His right hand in the heavenly places, far above all principality and power and might and dominion, and every name that is named, not only in this age but also in that which is to come. And He put all things under His feet,* ***and gave Him to be head*** *over all things to the* ***church, which is His body****, the fullness of Him who fills all in all.*
>
> Ephesians 1:20-23

Let's connect two verses of 1 Corinthians 12, Paul's chapter on spiritual gifts. Verse 12 reads, 'For as the body is one and has many members, but all the members of that one body, being many, are one body, so also is Christ'. And verse 27 reads, 'Now you are the body of Christ and members individually'.

On earth Jesus had one physical body. Now as the head in heaven he has a multi-membered, global body functioning just as he would if he was physically present himself, because by the anointing he is present!

Whatever is in the head – Christ – flows into the body which is the church; his thoughts, his will, his power and his love. The body is the extension of the head. The church, the body of Christ, experiences the same mission, the same anointing and the same ministry as Jesus. We speak and act in the name of Jesus because we are doing his works, to fulfil his mission in the power of the Spirit.

The same mission

When Jesus, rose from the dead, he appeared to his disciples and spoke these words, '"Peace to you! As the Father has sent Me, I also send you." And when He had said this, He breathed on them, and said to them, "Receive the Holy Spirit"' (John 20:21-22). They were commissioned just as he was. Jesus repeated and elaborated this further in what we know as The Great Commission in Matthew 28.

> *Then the eleven disciples went away into Galilee, to the mountain which Jesus had appointed for them. When they saw Him, they worshiped Him; but some doubted. And Jesus came and spoke to them, saying, "All authority has been given to me in heaven and on earth. Go therefore and make disciples of all the nations, baptizing them in the name of the Father and of the Son and of the Holy Spirit, teaching them to observe all things that I have commanded you; and lo, I am with you always, even to the end of the age."*
>
> Matthew 28:16-20

The return of Jesus to his Father's throne in heaven triggered the outpouring of the Holy Spirit on the Day of Pentecost. Since that time, God has not withdrawn his Spirit from the earth and has no intention of doing so until the work of God is completed; the harvest is reaped, the nations are won for Christ and the glory of God is manifest in the world.

Whatever mission the Father gave to Jesus, you can be sure that God has destined the church to follow suit. Whatever he was sent to do in that anointing, he transfers to the church, his body. You may struggle with the idea that you have the same mission as Jesus but we must realise that whatever God introduces into the earth he does not withdraw. Jesus came to win the world to himself. The church has been commissioned to nothing less than continuing in this same mission.

The same anointing

The world can only be rescued through an anointed church. The demonic ideologies we see active in the world will not be destroyed through argument alone. We live in a day when the meaning of truth itself is disputed. Isaiah described the culture of his day like this, 'Justice is turned back, and righteousness stands far away; for truth has stumbled in the public squares, and uprightness cannot enter' (Isaiah 59:14). What a description of our world today.

When you and I are anointed by the Holy Spirit we look the same as Jesus in the sight of God. We are his representatives, we re-present him to the world. This is why Jesus urged the disciples to wait in Jerusalem until they were 'clothed with power from on high'. They dare not step forth into a hostile world without first being equipped with the power to combat the demonic forces of darkness, the antagonistic religious authorities and the prevailing philosophies of the day.

Three things happened to the disciples concurrently on the Day of Pentecost:

- They were all baptized with the Holy Spirit, Acts 1:5
- They were all filled with the Holy Spirit, Acts 2:4
- They were all anointed with the Holy Spirit, Acts 1:8

These were the three components of one mighty event. We can therefore categorically say that when the disciples were baptized with the Holy Spirit they were anointed by him. The Holy Spirit came upon them in power. Paul describes the Holy Spirit working in him in the following way: 'For this I toil, struggling with all his energy that he powerfully works within me' (Colossians 1:29). The Holy Spirit gives us a spiritual energy on the inside of us.

The anointing of the Spirit has not been given as a recreational pleasure for believers but an empowering presence in their lives. We are his vessels and instruments, conducting his power from heaven to earth. The world will be won through every person living in the anointing of the Spirit, committed to Spirit filled churches and demonstrating Christ in and through their lives.

The same ministry

In John 14:12 Jesus declares, 'Most assuredly, I say to you, he who believes in me, the works that I do he will do also; and greater works than these he will do, because I go to My Father' (John 14:12-13). We have been given the same ministry as Jesus in order to fulfil the same mission as his and this is conducted in the power of the Spirit.

It is vital for believers to come to terms with the fact that God had no intention of reducing the power level when the Spirit was transferred from his Son to his church. One is the continuation of the other. To fulfil the same ministry as Christ requires the same power as Christ. Whatever is purposed in the head (Christ), is actioned in the body (the church).

The Holy Spirit coming on the church was no less than the continuation of Christ's ministry on the earth. I like to put it like this:

The Holy Spirit in the church is Jesus in the world!

To God the father, you and I look just like Jesus when we are anointed with the Holy Spirit. From the Day of Pentecost the early church began to minister in exactly the same way as Jesus did, doing the same works, speaking the same words.

The anointing of the Spirit on a believer can take a multitude of forms and outlets. As you read these words, consider what God has called and anointed you to do in life. Now realise that whatever you have been anointed to do, it is contributing to the same basic purpose; the salvation of men and women, freedom from Satan's oppression, total healing of body, soul and spirit and the advance of God's kingdom. Here is a simple principle for life; begin to do the works Jesus did and you will soon discover whatever else God has prepared for you to do in life.

The New Testament letters contain several lists of ministry gifts and callings, including things like 'administration', 'serving' and 'giving' as well as gifts like healing, prophecy and miracles. The point is that serving God embraces a vast spectrum of activities and ministries and they can and should all be operated in by the power of the Holy Spirit.

When Jesus returns

I want to finish this chapter by addressing the issue of the return of Jesus to usher in the kingdom of God in all its fullness. Where does this fit in with the idea that God is still working a grand centuries-old agenda to redeem planet earth? Which is true? Is the return of Christ around the corner or do we plan for the long term future?

The issue is resolved by holding these two truths in tension with each other. Jesus could indeed return at any time and we should live constantly in the light of his coming. 'Therefore you also be ready, for the Son of Man is coming at an hour you do not expect' (Matthew 24:44). This present evil age is passing away and the age to come is rapidly approaching. If the last days began two thousand years ago, we are closer than ever to the return of Christ.

Equally, we are here for a purpose and Jesus will not return until that purpose is fulfilled. Evangelical Christianity has been guilty of what has been termed 'the great retreat' – withdrawing from active engagement in society while we wait for the rapture of believers from planet earth! It is like football players facing their opponents on the field of play, but speculating on when the referee will blow his whistle rather than on scoring goals.

As a young believer I was easily influenced by the many Bible prophecy books and teachings all confidently predicting that the return of Jesus was just around the corner. Now more than 50 years later, none of those confident prophecies have been fulfilled but in the meantime the world is still here needing to be loved and reached with the gospel. The older I get, the more concerned I am for multi-generational planning while living ready for his coming at any time. There is no room for complacency in either direction.

4

The Year of Jubilee

On the 1st January 1863, as the United States of America approached its third year of bloody civil war, President Abraham Lincoln issued the Emancipation Proclamation. The proclamation declared that, *'All persons held as slaves within the rebellious states are, and henceforward shall be free'.* Overnight the legal status of 3.5 million people in the USA was changed. For up to 75,000 slaves, this meant immediate liberation. They lived in Union States and enjoyed the experience of freedom not just the status of freedom. For the remaining millions, the enjoyment of their freedom involved the winning of a war of liberation which was to take several more years.

The people of Israel were also liberated slaves. They had been held in Egypt for 400 hundred years until their exodus under the leadership of Moses. On entering the Promised Land, God wanted to ensure not one of them ever endured slavery again and so the Year of Jubilee was inaugurated. It is one of the most powerful prophetic teachings in the Bible and we read about it in the book of Leviticus chapter 25.

In my introduction I explained that the anointing of the Holy Spirit will always do one of two things – it will either liberate a person or equip them to liberate others. The Year of Jubilee is all about the first part of the equation – it is the Magna Carta of our freedom and we are going to explore what that means. The Year of Jubilee is a prophetic announcement of the liberty the anointing brings to men and women in Christ.

> *It shall come to pass in that day that his burden will be taken away from your shoulder, and his yoke from your neck, and the yoke will be destroyed because of the anointing oil.*
>
> Isaiah 10:27

The anointing breaks the yoke of Satan's bondage. The Year of Jubilee explains it. This wonderful provision was given to the people of Israel as part of the Law of Moses but it didn't remain in the Old Covenant. The Jubilee is directly fulfilled in Christ himself and his ministry. It then forms the basis for the ministry of the church. As with the emancipation of American slaves, our liberation in Christ comes in two parts. The blood of Christ gives us our *legal* freedom. The Spirit of Christ gives us our *experience* of freedom. But let's take this one step at a time.

In the Year of Jubilee God built into the nation of Israel a mechanism to ensure that whatever personal calamity might befall his people, they would not lose their property or their liberty or their family. Leviticus chapter 25 describes this in some detail and I encourage you to read the whole chapter. Here are the key verses.

> *And you shall count seven Sabbaths of years for yourself, seven times seven years; and the time of the seven Sabbaths of years shall be to you forty-nine years. Then you shall cause the trumpet of the Jubilee to sound on the tenth day of the seventh month; on the Day of Atonement you shall make the trumpet to sound throughout all your land. And you shall consecrate the fiftieth year, and proclaim liberty throughout all the land to all its inhabitants. It shall be a Jubilee for you; and each of you shall return to*

his possession, and each of you shall return to his family. That fiftieth year shall be a Jubilee to you.

Leviticus 25:8-11

The year of Jubilee was God's promise that his people would never be slaves again like they had been in Egypt. They would never be poor again. They would never be disinherited. Freedom and prosperity was built in to the nation. It was the heart of God at that time; it is the heart of God today. Concerning the Old Covenant writings the apostle Paul said, 'Whatever things were written before were written for our learning' (Romans 15:4). We can be sure the teaching of the Year of Jubilee is there for us.

The Jubilee took place every 50 years. The trumpet would sound on the 10th day of the 7th month, the Day of Atonement in the 49th year, and liberty would be proclaimed across the land. The trumpet that was blown was not the ram's horn trumpet, the *shofar*, but the silver trumpet called the *yobel* in Hebrew. Our word 'Jubilee' comes from this word *yobel*. Debts were cancelled, slaves set free. Families would be reunited. Those who lost their inheritance could reclaim it. There would be celebration everywhere. What an incredible day that would have been!

It would appear that Israel never properly kept their Jubilee once they entered the Promised Land. But despite that, God had a greater prophetic purpose wrapped up in the principle of the Jubilee because the Year of Jubilee was fulfilled in and through Jesus Christ. There is now a timeless reality that Jesus is our Jubilee and we are going to see how this came about.

First of all though, we need to understand the year of Jubilee itself. What did it consist of? The Year of Jubilee contained one purpose and two core principles. It was then applied through four provisions and every component of this prophetic teaching is now fulfilled in Christ, our living year of Jubilee.

One Purpose

Hundreds of years after the Jubilee was given by Moses, Isaiah the prophet declared the following words in anticipation of the coming of the Messiah. They are nothing short of a Jubilee proclamation. Isaiah took the truth of the Leviticus Jubilee and elevated it to a new spiritual level declaring that it will be fulfilled in the coming of the messiah.

> *The Spirit of the Lord GOD is upon me, because the LORD has anointed me to bring good news to the poor; he has sent me to bind up the brokenhearted, to proclaim liberty to the captives, and the opening of the prison to those who are bound; to proclaim the year of the LORD'S favor, and the day of vengeance of our God.*
>
> Isaiah 61:1-2

The prophet Isaiah caught the spiritual significance of the Year of Jubilee, a restoration of the total person, spirit, soul and body. God was going to restore to men and women all that had been lost because of Satan and sin. Furthermore, this would not be limited to the Jewish nation alone, it was open to everyone. This spiritual Jubilee would introduce full salvation to all of mankind through Jesus Christ.

Now fast forward another 700 years and we find Jesus entering the synagogue in his home town of Nazareth and reading Isaiah's words. Let's remind ourselves of the precise sequence of events. Prior to his water baptism, Jesus had performed no miracle. At the age of thirty he presented himself to John the Baptist and was baptized by John in the Jordan. As he emerged out of the water, the Holy Spirit descended on him and from that day he was anointed for ministry.

Jesus is then led by the Spirit into the wilderness to be tempted by the devil for forty days. Having overcome Satan he then returns to Galilee in the anointing power of the Spirit and after an initial season of ministry, enters the synagogue in Nazareth where the scroll of Isaiah the prophet is handed to him. He opens the scroll and reads the passage from chapter 61. Luke records what followed:

> *Then He closed the book, and gave it back to the attendant and sat down. And the eyes of all who were in the synagogue were fixed on Him. And He began to say to them, "Today this Scripture is fulfilled in your hearing."*
>
> Luke 4:20-21

Jesus was literally owning the prophecy of Isaiah and declaring with authority that the Holy Spirit had anointed him to bring spiritual, moral, economic and social liberation to men and women. He came to inaugurate a program of Jubilee. He was saying, **'I am the Jubilee. I am what this is all about. I came to bring liberty, recovery and restoration to mankind; spirit, soul and body'.**

During his earthly ministry Jesus literally fulfilled this Jubilee mandate in the way Isaiah 61 describes. But this ministry didn't end with the death of Christ, in fact the opposite. It was his death and resurrection that enabled this Jubilee ministry to be carried forward into the early disciples and then multiplied throughout the church.

The ascension of Jesus to the right hand of the father signaled the point at which the Jubilee mandates were handed to the church to continue the ministry of Jesus. Because when Jesus arrived at the throne of God the Holy Spirit was poured out upon the waiting church in Jerusalem. I have summarized the truth of the Jubilee in its stages in the table below.

Jubilee Bible reference	Jubilee Significance
Leviticus 25:1-55	Given to Israel by Moses
Isaiah 61:1-3	Prophesied by Isaiah
Luke 4:14-21	Fulfilled in Christ
John 14:12, Acts 1:8	Transmitted to the church

Two Principles

The Year of Jubilee not only contained one purpose, it was based on two principles. Just as with the one purpose, so the two principles are fulfilled in Christ and then transmitted to his people today through the salvation he obtained for us at the cross. What are those two principles?

1. The people belonged to God by redemption, verse 42, 55.

   For they (God's people Israel) are my servants, whom I brought out of the land of Egypt; they shall not be sold as slaves.

   Leviticus 25:42

The Year of Jubilee was a perpetual reminder that God had redeemed a people out of slavery in Egypt and brought them across the Red Sea, through the wilderness and into their Promised Land. Furthermore the year of Jubilee was announced on the Day of Atonement (Leviticus 25:9). Once a year on the Day of Atonement the blood of a bull and a goat was brought into the Holy of Holies behind the veil and sprinkled onto the mercy seat of God's presence to 'make atonement' for sin. The English word 'atonement' means oneness or literally 'at-one-ment'. It was coined in the English language during the 15th

Century but it was William Tyndale who popularized it in his 1525 English translation of the Bible to translate the Hebrew word 'kippir' for which there was no other English word available.

Deliverance from Egypt and the Day of Atonement are examples of how the Old Testament is fulfilled in Christ, especially in his death and resurrection. Everything Jesus has provided for us to enjoy finds its source at the cross. When Jesus died and rose again, freedom was secured. When the Holy Spirit was poured out on the Day of Pentecost the Jubilee mandates were transmitted to the church his body, for them to continue in the earth.

2. The land belonged to God by creation, verse 23.

> *The land shall not be sold permanently, for the land is mine; for you are strangers and sojourners with me. And in all the land of your possession you shall grant redemption of the land.*
>
> Leviticus 25:23-24

Not only were the people of Israel God's possession by redemption, the land was God's by creation. In the Year of Jubilee the peoples' land and property were restored. What does the Promised Land really signify for us? Why is it important? The land was the inheritance given by God to his people. Leviticus 25 ensured that people could return to their property in the Jubilee. They could claim back their inheritance. In the fulfillment of the Year of Jubilee the 'Promised Land' is everything God has given to his redeemed people, everything lost through sin and the fall.

When Adam fell into sin he lost his dignity, his authority and his position of dominion. He became subject to sin, sickness, poverty and death. But all that changed in the death and resurrection of Christ. The Year of Jubilee was a prophetic statement of God's will in Christ, namely that our Inheritance is restored. Now in Christ you and I get back what God gave us in the first place. Every believer needs to know what belongs to them by covenant right and experience the blessings of salvation.

Four provisions

The Year of Jubilee contained four provisions for God's people. When Jesus stood in the synagogue in Nazareth and read from Isaiah 61, he finished by stating, 'Today this Scripture is fulfilled in your hearing' (verse 21). Now let's look at how Jesus took the year of Jubilee and fulfilled it in himself. Here are the mandates Jesus announced in the synagogue that day in Nazareth.

> *"The Spirit of the Lord is upon me, because he has anointed me to proclaim good news to the poor. He has sent me to proclaim liberty to the captives and recovering of sight to the blind, to set at liberty those who are oppressed, to proclaim the year of the Lord's favour."*
>
> Luke 4:18-19 ESV

It was as if Jesus was taking the silver trumpet to his lips and sounding the prophetic note that the Jubilee had arrived. His anointing to liberate men and women from Satan's power was summarized in four statements quoted from Isaiah 61. There is some variation in the way these verses are translated and the order of Jesus' statements but if we overlay Luke 4:18-19 onto Isaiah 61:1-2 we see a perfect picture of how Christ fulfils each statement.

Jubilee provisions (Leviticus 25)	**Fulfilled in Christ (Isaiah 61 and Luke 4)**
Debts cancelled, verses 25-28, 47-54	Good news for the poor
Slaves released, verses 35-36	Liberty to the captives
Property returned, verses 23-24	Recovery of sight to the blind
Relationships restored, verses 10, 41	Healing the broken-hearted

Number one – Good news for the poor

In the Year of Jubilee debts were cancelled and as a result those who had become economic slaves were released and every other benefit and blessing of the Jubilee could be experienced. It made no difference who you were or how you came into debt, whether your creditor was an Israelite or a foreigner, when the trumpet sounded your debts were cancelled. At the Jubilee God drew a line and said, *'No more! They are my people and they are free.'* This provision of cancelled debts is so powerful and wonderful.

I am convinced that when Jesus said that he came to announce good news for the poor, he was referring to forgiveness, the cancelling of the debt of sins. 'The poor' are those who are humble and convicted of their sin and their need of a saviour. The 'good news' is the provision of salvation through faith in Jesus Christ. It is a reminder of Jesus' words in Matthew 5:3, 'Blessed are the poor in spirit for theirs is the kingdom of God'. Entrance to God's kingdom is available for the humble and repentant.

Now it is essential to see that this is an anointed ministry of the Holy Spirit. Jesus said, 'the Spirit of the Lord is upon me because he has anointed me to preach good news to the poor' (Luke 4:18). We can express it like this:

- Our salvation was secured at the cross by the blood of the Son of God
- Our salvation is applied at conversion by the anointing of the Spirit of God

Salvation through Christ is a two-part work. Christ secured it legally for us at the cross through the shedding of his blood. But we experience it by a work of the Holy Spirit. When the gospel is preached in the power of the Holy Spirit he applies those truths to the human heart and the result is the new birth. You don't have to be an Ephesians 4 evangelist to operate in this anointing, simply sharing Christ and your personal testimony of salvation will break the yoke of bondage and set people free from their sin.

Do you realise it made no difference how the people of Israel lost their inheritance. The Jubilee put it all right again. We are inclined to think God will treat us in proportion to what we deserve. But he treats us according to how Jesus has provided for us. The Jubilee brought everyone back up to the fullest level, no matter how far down they had fallen or how they got there. This restoration was not based on anything the people did whatsoever. It was based on the free gift of God's grace. It was God's covenant provision in the atonement. When the trumpet sounded you went home. Now because Jesus paid the price of sin in full at the cross, the child of God can receive every other benefit of salvation just as the people of Israel enjoyed the full benefits of the Jubilee. That is what comes next.

Number two – Liberty to the captives

The people had been slaves in Egypt but God delivered them and now they belonged to him. It was inconceivable that God's liberated people should be forced to serve anyone else. In the Jubilee freedom from slavery was secured through the cancelling of debts. What does this mean for you and me? When your sins are forgiven you are legally entitled to enjoy freedom from the power of sin and freedom from all demonic oppression.

- Freedom from the power of sin

Christian freedom is an incredible experience. Through the blood of Jesus the debt of our sins is cancelled and through the cross of Christ the power of sin is broken. I remember the day this revelation came to me as a young believer struggling to live victoriously over sexual temptation along with a host of other issues. I read Watchman Nee's book 'The Normal Christian Life'. He describes the way the cross of Christ has liberated us from the power of sin just as the blood of Christ has cancelled the penalty of sin. Watchman Nee bases his teaching on Romans chapter 6 and describes three steps to experiencing this freedom:

> ***Knowing this**, that our old man was crucified with Him, that the body of sin might be done away with, that we should no longer be slaves of sin.*
>
> Romans 6:6

The first step to freedom is to **know** the absolute truth that when Christ died, you died with him and when he rose from the dead, you rose with him. This is revelation knowledge not head knowledge. When you receive this truth as God's word it will penetrate your spirit and revelation knowledge will become the truth in your heart!

> *Likewise you also,* ***reckon*** *yourselves to be dead indeed to sin, but alive to God in Christ Jesus our Lord.*
>
> Romans 6:11

The second step is to then **reckon** yourself dead to sin and alive to God. Another word used is to **count** yourself dead to sin and alive to God. It means to apply this truth to yourself, account for it in your personal bank account. Conclude that this truth is actually and personally yours to know and it will be yours in experience.

> *And do not present your members as instruments of unrighteousness to sin, but* ***present yourselves to God*** *as being alive from the dead, and your members as instruments of righteousness to God.*
>
> Romans 6:13-14

Finally Watchman Nee explains that you must **present your body** and its members to God as a slave would present themselves to their master. God did not break your chains to leave you free-wheeling around. You become bound to him and he protects you. When you present yourself and the members of your body to Christ you literally submit them to him and bring them under his Lordship. Embedding this truth in your heart will bring a definite experience of freedom to you as it did to me.

- Freedom from demonic oppression.

The reality of a personal devil is inescapable. We saw his role in the downfall of Adam and Eve in the garden. We also saw how Jesus came to destroy his works on the cross.

> *. . . For this purpose the Son of God was manifested, that He might destroy the works of the devil.*
>
> 1 John 3:8

The word John uses here for 'destroy' is *luo*, which means to unravel rather than annihilate. At the cross, Jesus gained the decisive victory over Satan, he unraveled him, and when Christ returns Satan will be cast into the lake of fire according to Revelation 21. In the meantime he is still active operating through a hierarchy of demonic personalities as Paul explains in Ephesians chapter 6:10-20.

I have been confronted by the reality of demonized people many times and not just in places like Africa or India but in the UK too. My first experience took place when I was just 18 years old while on an evangelistic mission in Wiltshire, England. The mission team were praying together with a young lady who was trapped in terrible darkness. She and her sister had become deeply involved in the occult including telekinesis, Ouija boards and levitation. This young lady had literally been levitated by demonic power.

As we prayed, the demons afflicting her began to get very agitated. Her face contorted and she began writhing on the floor. We in turn began to speak and sing in tongues all together. A demon shrieked out *'Not that! Anything but that!'* Suddenly the girl rushed toward me and I instinctively rebuked the evil spirit in the name of Jesus. There was immediate relief. The demons fled and she was freed through God's power and the authority invested in the name of Jesus. Subsequently she surrendered her life fully to Christ and repented of past occult activity.

However powerful demons may appear to be, the believer has been given authority over all their strategies. This is our legal position in Christ. It simply remains for every believer to walk in a life that pleases God, stand in the armour we have been given and resist every enemy assault. James 4:7 says '. . . submit to God, resist the devil and he will flee from you'. It is the absolute birthright of every believer to live free from demonic oppression of any kind.

Number three – Recovery of sight to the blind

'Recovery of sight to the blind' is a motif for physical healing of every kind and it is clear from Jesus' own earthly ministry that he came to heal all kinds of sickness. This is a direct prophetic fulfilment of the Jubilee and is represented as such by the restoration of property. Property was the peoples' inheritance. That is exactly what healing is, a restoration of our inheritance.

> *And Jesus went about all Galilee, teaching in their synagogues, preaching the gospel of the kingdom, and healing all kinds of sickness and all kinds of disease among the people.*
>
> Matthew 4:23

There is so much we could say about divine healing and the believer's authority both to receive and to minister healing today. However, the most important issue at stake is to know the basis for healing – it is in the cross of Christ. Just as restoration of property was connected to cancelling of debts, so too healing is connected to forgiveness of sins. Isaiah's reference to the atoning death of messiah makes that crystal clear.

> *Surely He has borne our griefs and carried our sorrows; yet we esteemed Him stricken, smitten by God, and afflicted. But He was wounded for our transgressions, he was bruised for our iniquities; the*

> *chastisement for our peace was upon Him,* ***and by His stripes we are healed.***
>
> Isaiah 53:4-5

Healing is absolutely central to the gospel. Jesus healed the sick throughout his ministry. It went right alongside preaching the gospel just as restoration of property went right alongside cancelling debts in the Jubilee. Forgiveness of sins and healing of sickness sit together and both have their source in the cross of Christ.

Our gospel is good news of full salvation. It provides healing of bruised hearts, broken relationships dashed hopes and sick bodies. Where people have been ravaged and blighted by Satan, the grace of God restores fully and freely. Healing is therefore a ministry of the anointed Christ who then commissioned the disciples to heal the sick in his name. Finally the Holy Spirit anointed the church on the Day of Pentecost to continue to heal the sick.

God has anointed you and me with the same healing anointing as Jesus. Yes, the Bible recognises the particular ministry of healing the sick given to some but it is also for all believers. 'And these signs will follow those who believe: In My name they will . . . lay hands on the sick, and they will recover' (Mark 16:17-18).

Number four – Healing the broken-hearted

In the Year of Jubilee relationships were restored. Jesus came to fulfil this wonderful prophetic picture when he declared he had come to 'heal the broken-hearted'. Human hearts and lives are broken through family break-down, divorce, betrayal, abuse, cruelty and a host of other social ills. We see the evidence of this everywhere in society today. It is impossible to quantify the extent of the damage to people young and old through broken and dysfunctional relationships.

The healing of the human heart is possibly the most neglected area of ministry in the church today and yet it formed one of the four mandates of Jesus' anointing. We have to understand that sin not only separated men and women from God, it has crushed and bruised human hearts ever since. Therefore the gospel is not only the anointing to reconcile man to God but to restore them from the damage and harm inflicted on them. Jesus came to heal all who have been emotionally and mentally damaged and scarred.

LifeSpring churches hold the truth of heart healing as a core value and we have witnessed countless lives transformed and relationships restored by the power of God's love. The fact is, healing of the broken-hearted was a major part of Jesus' ministry mandate. We do well to elevate it in our churches and ministries. Nothing has changed in 2,000 years, men and women need to experience wholeness and healing from the damage to their souls as much today as ever.

Jubilee Today

Now God has not limited this Jubilee ministry to Jesus alone. God has entrusted the same mission to the church. If there is one message I want to convey in this book it is that we have been commissioned by Christ to bring salvation and liberation to the world. The church has been entrusted with the ministry of the Jubilee. Look back at Isaiah 61 with me for a moment and notice what becomes of those who are liberated by the Jubilee anointing.

> *And they shall rebuild the old ruins, they shall raise up the former desolations, and they shall repair the ruined cities, the desolations of many generations.*
>
> Isaiah 61:4

The ones who were mourning and desolate in verse 3 become the ones restoring, rebuilding and renewing in verse 4. The anointing of the Spirit sets the captives free so that they take that anointing and set other captives free. That is you and I, filled with the Holy Spirit continuing where Jesus left off.

If you are just beginning to really comprehend this amazing truth I want you to pause right now and say this prayer out loud:

> *Father I thank you that you have set me free by the power of the Holy Spirit, from sin, sickness, sadness and death. You have broken my chains of oppression. Jesus has made me free and free indeed. Now I present my body soul and spirit to you, a living sacrifice for you to fill me and use me to your glory to set others free by the same anointing that was on your son Jesus. Fill me afresh as I present myself to you today, Amen!*

Above and beyond anything else, God has anointed the church to preach Christ in the power of the Spirit. As soon as you open your mouth to share your personal testimony or the truths of the gospel, the Holy Spirit empowers your words and human hearts become receptive to their saviour. We must understand how motivated the Holy Spirit is to back up our words with his anointing.

5

Othniel, the first anointed man on earth

It's time to look at an incredible Bible character who I refer to as the first anointed person to ever walk the earth. The law of first mention is a very important principle of Scripture recognizing that the first time we encounter a particular subject in Scripture we can observe principles that define that subject wherever else we find it. The first person to experience the anointing is therefore very important. He appears in the book of Judges.

The time of the Judges was unique. It begins after Joshua led the people to possess their inheritance in Canaan and ends with Saul son of Kish being appointed as the first king of Israel. Between these bookends of time lived the judges. This was a new administration of God's purposes, unseen before. During this time God navigated his people safely through the threats and strategies of the enemy by the hands of judges – or more aptly deliverers – until God's people Israel was positioned for the advent of the kingdom of David.

The time of the Judges was in fact a downward spiral for the people of God and the national life of Israel. After entering the Promised Land, all went well under the leadership of Joshua and his contemporaries but soon after the death of Joshua the people drifted into backsliding and idolatry. Here is how the Book of Judges describes what happened next:

> *Now Joshua the son of Nun, the servant of the LORD, died when he was one hundred and ten years old. And they buried him within the border of his inheritance at Timnath Heres, in the mountains of Ephraim, on the north side of Mount Gaash. When all that generation had been gathered to their fathers, another generation arose after them who did not know the LORD nor the work which He had done for Israel. Then the children of Israel did evil in the sight of the LORD, and served the Baals; and they forsook the LORD God of their fathers, who had brought them out of the land of Egypt; and they followed other gods from among the gods of the people who were all around them, and they bowed down to them; and they provoked the LORD to anger.*
>
> Judges 2:8-12

From then on cycles of backsliding and restoration dominated the next 400 years. As a consequence of their backsliding, God sold Israel into the hands of their enemies who cruelly oppressed them. In their distress the people cried out to God and in response he raised up the judges who led them to overthrow their oppressors. Peace and prosperity was restored once more and the people enjoyed the good times until the process of backsliding ensued again.

The ministry of the judges was accompanied by supernatural signs, wonders and miracles. Sometimes they were assisted in battle by direct help from heaven, with remarkable and unusual results. An army with 900 chariots was defeated by a rain storm (Judges 5:21). Gideon's tiny army of 300 defeated the entire Midianite army along with their camels (Judges 7:19-25). Shamgar killed 600 Philistines with an Ox goad (Judges 4:31). And so it goes on.

The age of the anointing

The period of the Judges represented a season unlike anything that had come before. God did something completely new; he visited personally upon a man or a woman by His Holy Spirit and as a consequence that person performed extraordinary deeds. It can be summed up in one word – the anointing. There had been great leaders, prophets and spiritual fathers before this time of course. Abraham was a mighty man of faith and father of all who believe. Moses led the people of Israel out of Egypt. Joshua led the conquest of the land. But what came next was completely new. I am not diminishing these previous spiritual giants in the slightest but none of them were described as anointed by the Holy Spirit in the way we see in the book of Judges.

The Holy Spirit is clearly present and active before the time of the Judges. For example, a man called Bezalel was hand-picked by God for the task of building the Tabernacle in the wilderness and equipped for that task by the Holy Spirit.

> *Then the LORD spoke to Moses, saying: "See, I have called by name Bezalel the son of Uri, the son of Hur, of the tribe of Judah. And I have filled him with the Spirit of God, in wisdom, in understanding, in knowledge, and in all manner of workmanship, to design artistic works, to work in gold, in silver, in bronze, in cutting jewels for setting, in carving wood, and to work in all manner of workmanship.*
>
> Exodus 31:1-5

But in the book of Judges we read expressions like, *'The Spirit came upon Gideon'* or *'The Spirit rushed mightily upon Samson'.* We do not find such descriptions before the time of the Judges.

This new administration of the Holy Spirit had ramifications for the powers of darkness. The devil had never witnessed anything like this before. Remember that from the time the prophecy was issued in Genesis chapter 3, the devil was on the look-out for whoever the seed of the woman might be that would possibly destroy him. This person would be the anointed deliverer, the saviour or messiah of God's people. So the appearance of these anointed Judges put Satan on high alert. An activity of the Spirit of God on men and women was breaking out and Satan was alarmed.

Of all the judges that God raised up there were in fact only four specifically described as experiencing the Holy Spirit coming upon them in power. It may well be that all of them were anointed. Descriptions of their activities would lead us to believe that is the case, but only four are described in this way. In reverse chronological order they are as follows:

Number 4 was Samson. He was the final anointed judge and he was unique. God raised him up at the end of this period to defeat Israel's arch enemy the Philistines. I am going to devote a whole chapter to Samson but for now it is good to be aware that he experienced the supernatural power of God like none before or after.

Before Samson there was Jephthah, who came from the tribe of the Gileadites who lived on the Eastern side of the Jordan. Jephthah was a highly unusual individual, flawed in many ways but used by God none the less to deliver the people of Israel from the Ammonites.

Coming in at number 2 was Gideon of whom I have devoted a whole book, 'How to Come Back Strong'. I recommend you read this book in order to gain a true perspective of a much misunderstood and misrepresented man of God. Along with his brothers, Gideon was a resistance fighter, giving the Midianites a rough time during their oppression of Israel. Gideon defeated the Midianites in spectacular fashion and went on to judge Israel for a further 20 years.

Finally we come to the very first person to experience the anointing of the Holy Spirit. This was a man by the name of Othniel – the first recorded person in history upon whom the Spirit of God descended in power. What must that have looked like? How did he feel when the Spirit of God came upon him? There was no precedent for it. There was no reference point for it. Othniel must have thought, *'what just happened'*. Everything changed with the advent of Othniel. The irony is that no one ever speaks about him. I have never heard a sermon preached on Othniel or a book written about him. I intend to put that right because God has something special to say through this man.

Enter Othniel

The passage in the book of Judges in which Othniel first appears is brief. Perhaps that is why he has been so overlooked! Here it is:

> *So the children of Israel did evil in the sight of the LORD. They forgot the LORD their God, and served the Baals and Asherahs. Therefore the anger of the LORD was hot against Israel, and He sold them into the hand of Cushan-Rishathaim king of Mesopotamia; and the children of Israel served Cushan-Rishathaim eight years. When the children of Israel cried out to the LORD, the LORD raised up a deliverer for the children of Israel, who delivered them: Othniel the son of Kenaz, Caleb's younger brother. The Spirit of the LORD came upon him, and he judged Israel. He went out to war, and the LORD delivered Cushan-Rishathaim king of*

> *Mesopotamia into his hand; and his hand prevailed over Cushan-Rishathaim. So the land had rest for forty years. Then Othniel the son of Kenaz died.*
>
> Judges 3:7-11

Othniel was the first judge and the first anointed deliverer, the prototype or model for those who followed. What was special about him that God chose him to pioneer such a new way of working? God is careful who he chooses. Something must have attracted God's attention. What was it? Can we find out? Yes, because before he appears in the Book of Judges, we read about his life in the Book of Joshua:

> *Now to Caleb the son of Jephunneh he (Joshua) gave a share among the children of Judah, according to the commandment of the LORD to Joshua, namely, Kirjath Arba, which is Hebron (Arba was the father of Anak). Caleb drove out the three sons of Anak from there: Sheshai, Ahiman, and Talmai, the children of Anak. Then he went up from there to the inhabitants of Debir (formerly the name of Debir was Kirjath Sepher). And Caleb said, "He who attacks Kirjath Sepher and takes it, to him I will give Achsah my daughter as wife." So Othniel the son of Kenaz, the brother of Caleb, took it; and he gave him Achsah his daughter as wife. Now it was so, when she came to him, that she persuaded him to ask her father for a field. So she dismounted from her donkey, and Caleb said to her, "What do you wish?" She answered, "Give me a blessing; since you have given me land in the South, give me also springs of water." So he gave her the upper springs and the lower springs.*
>
> Joshua 15:13-19

This passage is important. It reveals things about Othniel's character that explain why God chose him. The anointing is no accident. We don't just fall into the power of the Holy Spirit like a game of chance. God was very careful in his choice of who would experience the anointing. I don't believe this has changed. I have identified 3 defining features for today's anointed sons and daughters that align with those of Othniel. We need to rediscover them and they are right there for us in plain sight. They are keys for you and I to walk in our anointing too.

Number one – Othniel dealt with his identity issues

Othniel's father was Kenaz the brother of Caleb. We know only two of the original people who came out of Israel eventually entered the Promised Land, Joshua and Caleb. So Othniel's father did not enter Canaan. Sadly he was among the unbelieving company who perished in the wilderness with the rest of his generation.

But Othniel did not allow this fact to rob him of a blessed life and fulfilled destiny. He refused to be the unbelieving son of an unbelieving father. Instead he took inspiration from his uncle Caleb. On the inside Othniel must have said something like this, *'I will not be defined by my father's failure. My father may not have entered the land of promise but my uncle did. He will be my inspiration.'*

The role of fathers is crucial in affirming identity and developing destiny. Society has sadly reduced fatherhood to at best an accessory and at worst a toxic threat. The demise of fatherhood is at the root of countless social problems – this is well documented but unwelcome in a post-modern world that has consigned the role of men to little more than sperm donors for the new breed of alpha female. The sad reality is that countless men today have allowed an absent father, a negligent father, an abusive father, or a dysfunctional father to define them when there is no need for this to happen.

I love my own earthly father. He was a wonderful man and I had the privilege of leading him to Christ on his death bed. I miss him and look forward to being reunited with him in glory. But my father was also a broken man. I described earlier how he had endured 3 years as a Japanese prisoner in the Second World War. This experience had a devastating effect on him from which he never truly recovered.

By the time he returned home in November 1945 he had become reclusive and withdrawn. This is how I remember him; private and not particularly verbal. He loved his family and I loved and admired him immensely but he was not someone who affirmed me or inspired me to dream big, believe in myself and pursue life goals. Neither did he teach me the things of God or speak the promises of God over me. I had to come to the point in life where I took inspiration from what my heavenly Father said about me and discover what he had in store for me. This was a massive and at times painful journey.

Furthermore, God provided what I needed through inspirational spiritual fathers and mothers whom he brought into my life and to whom I owe a debt of gratitude. I looked at their lives. I listened to their words. I followed their ways. In turn they guided and affirmed me and through them I discovered that I do not need to be defined by my earthly father, family of friends. I am who God says I am and I can do what God says I can do. I will become what God says I will become. It is the same for you. In the words of Robert Schuller, you come to realise, *'If it's going to be, it's up to me'*.

Be an Othniel! Follow the fathers who inspire you and stir you. Two of the most inspirational people I ever met were Charles and Mary Clarke. They radiated the love of God and trained me in spiritual principles I walk in to this day. At the age of sixteen I met regularly with Charles who taught me the secrets of prayer and devotion to God. He was a retired Methodist minister and lifelong student of revival who inspired me to read and study the lives of the great revivalists for myself.

Let me finish this section by sharing one of the most important keys to gaining from spiritual fathers; you have to follow them! God will bring key people into your life, but when he does, don't just wait for them. They themselves know that the disciple does the following, not the teacher. So position your heart correctly for God to give you what you need. Here are three keys to positioning yourself to benefit from fathers in your life.

- Honour the spiritual fathers who have already been promoted to heaven. You can be fathered through the books and materials of past spiritual men and women of God. Honour these 'giants of the faith' by sitting at their feet as you study their lives. Devour their materials. It has never been easier to access such life-changing ministry, some of which has been around for centuries.
- Honour the living spiritual fathers through listening to their ministry, travelling to hear them preach and financially supporting their ministries. I am aware that the internet can be a can of worms. So be careful out there. Conversely, don't look for perfect people with squeaky clean theology. Look around for those who God is using on the global Christian stage, who are commended by other reputable ministries and who have a clear testimony.
- Honour the spiritual fathers you already have around you. We say this all the time in LifeSpring

churches. We aim to create an environment and culture of family, where spiritual fathers and mothers are within arm's length to anyone who is hungry enough to appreciate them. Honour what you already have and make the most of it and God will add more.

Number two – Othniel exercised courage to make the best choices

Achsah, the woman Othniel chose to marry was no stranger to him, she was the daughter of his uncle Caleb. He was very familiar with the quality of her heart and life. She was like her father Caleb. Othniel wanted that lady and when given the opportunity to take her in marriage he grabbed it at risk to his own life. Othniel's uncle Caleb had made an open invitation to anyone who would accept the challenge he offered. Whoever conquered the city of Kirath Sepher would have his daughter Achsah in marriage too. For Othniel it was a done deal. If it meant conquering a city in order to gain his uncle's daughter in marriage he would do it.

Have you ever wondered why some people seem to be luckier than others? Many studies have been conducted on this subject. The results are fascinating. Of course it has been realised there is a form of luck over which no one has power – the way the dice roll or a deck of cards is dealt. But there is a deeper kind of luck which is to do with the person themselves. What we refer to as luck is more commonly the combination of three ingredients.

- First there is a latent desire or inner attitude in the heart and mind of the person who seems to experience the luck. This disposes them to be constantly alert and expecting good to come their way. Their nose is sniffing. They are leaning in to the positive side of life. This is exactly how believers should live because they have a relationship with a good God who creates hope and faith within them.

- Secondly an opportunity comes their way. Because this aligns with the pre-disposition of their inner compass they are ready. They see what other don't. They recognise what has appeared in front of them as their moment to strike.
- Third they have the courage to act. They face the risks, take a deep breath and jump. That I believe is what marked Othniel out. And that defining hallmark of courage is what is needed in our generation as never before. It is what attracts the anointing.

The desires God places in our hearts come attached to the exercise of courage if they are ever to be experienced. Destiny lies beyond challenges that can only be overcome through courage. Nothing of any worth in this life is achieved without courage. There will never be a season or opportunity in life that you can navigate without courage. The greater the vision, the greater the courage needed to embrace it. The greater the threat, the greater the courage required to overcome it.

Courage like other virtues has been twisted and perverted in our age. As a word it has been tacked on to questionable behaviour in order to give it moral acceptance. You hear people talk like this today: 'the courage to put myself first', 'the courage to have an affair' or 'the courage to give up and quit.'

But the hallmark of courage is not taking the line of least resistance but rising up to do the noblest deed. Here is the hub of the matter. Courage is a character issue. To display courage is to demonstrate character. Courage requires personal sacrifice for the sake of a pre-eminent cause. Winston Churchill once said 'Courage is the greatest virtue because it makes all the other virtues possible'.

Here is a shocking truth; courage does not come from God, it comes from you! Courage is not a gift from God. It is something you take. Courage is not a gift from God but a command from God: Moses said to the people:

> *Be strong and of good courage, do not fear nor be afraid of them; for the LORD your God, He is the one who goes with you. He will not leave you nor forsake you.*
>
> Deuteronomy 31:6

After the death of Moses, God spoke these words to Joshua as he was about to lead the people across the Jordan River:

> *Be strong and of good courage, for to this people you shall divide as an inheritance the land which I swore to their fathers to give them.*
>
> Joshua 1:6

> *Have I not commanded you? Be strong and of good courage; do not be afraid, nor be dismayed, for the LORD your God is with you wherever you go.*
>
> Joshua 1:9

Courage is not the absence of fear. In fact you don't know courage until you are afraid. You cannot make the absence of fear the pre-condition for doing the will of God. The reason why the Bible constantly tells us to 'fear not' is precisely because we get afraid. The problem is not the presence of fear but the absence of courage. Courage is not a feeling. You can wait all you like for feelings of courage to arrive but let me save you the time, they won't come.

Let's look at the relationship between fear and courage more closely. Courage is not the absence of fear but a decision to act in spite of fear. In fact it is not courage until you feel the fear. Sometimes the only thing that separates you from your destiny is the decision to exercise courage. That is what Othniel had to do in stepping forward when the opportunity appeared. Fear is conquered through courage. Indeed the antidote to fear is courage. There is no deliverance from fear that avoids the application, at least in some measure, of courage. However helpful counselling, therapy and prayer may be, you will never bypass the need to act courageously.

After so many decades of pastoral ministry I have noticed that people don't instinctively pray for more courage but for less fear. They believe they need comfort not courage. But God doesn't make the devil weaker he makes you stronger. He intends for you to grow mighty in battle (Hebrews 11:34). In fact God has no plan to make the devil weaker or life easier – only to make you more resilient. Don't settle for comfort when God is offering you courage.

I believe courage is a major key to receiving the anointing. We can see this in the story of Gideon. After Gideon's encounter with the angel of the Lord, the first thing God required of Gideon was to tear down his father's altar to Baal. This required courage. God had just revealed himself as 'The Lord is Peace', YHWH SHALOM, but then he throws Gideon into the firing line! This supernatural peace is found in in the face of conflict.

Make no mistake, Gideon was afraid. We see that in Judges 6:27, which says he did this by night because he was afraid. Then God anointed Gideon straight afterwards (verse 34). The anointing to deliver a nation began with tearing down an altar to Baal in his back yard. In other words, a move of God rested on the shoulders of simple courage. The Holy Spirit loves courage.

It would be the same for Othniel. The courage he displayed in conquering the city of Kirath Sepher was the prelude for the anointing he received for delivering the nation. Finally it is the same for you and me. The moment you take courage for the step in front of you, God clothes you with everything else you need. Courage is the first move! Psalms 31:24 says: 'Be of good courage, and He shall strengthen your heart, all you who hope in the LORD.' When you exercise courage God will provide you with strength.

God cannot anoint fear, worry or cowardice. When you take courage, God gives you power. Don't hide behind false spirituality when action is required. Prayer is of course essential to spiritual power. Prayer puts a demand on God for the anointing. But at the same time, heaven puts a demand on man for courage and courage attracts the anointing!

Number three – Othniel was greedy for everything God had for him

Othniel's newly betrothed wife Achsah now pestered Othniel to ask her father for some land. 'Now it was so, when she came to him, that she persuaded him to ask her father for a field' (Joshua 15:18). So he asked and received. He didn't think, *'I should just be grateful and content with what I have been given'.* Caleb recognised a quality in Othniel when he made his request and was absolutely fine with him asking for more. A man of faith recognised another man of faith!

But it didn't stop there. Because after Othniel's success, Achsah herself then approached her father and asked him for springs of water. I am convinced that one reason God chose Othniel to receive his anointing was because he was greedy for all that was good, for all that God could give him. Othniel valued the principle of inheritance, whether his own or the whole nation of Israel. The blessing of God takes many forms and manifests itself in all kinds of ways. This includes spiritual, physical, emotional, relational and material blessing.

Psalm 37 verse 4 says, 'Delight yourself in the Lord and he will give you the desires of your heart'. Othniel received the wife he desired, the inheritance of land and now the springs of water to create prosperity. God saw that in Othniel was a warrior and a man who created a legacy and he chose him to be the first anointed judge of Israel.

As a young believer, I heard many fanciful things preached from the pulpit of my church that had no origin in the word of God. I had to learn to discern these myths and traditions and it wasn't always easy. I have already described the blessing of true spiritual fathers and mothers for which I thank God. But there were many not-so-helpful characters, some were men and women a lot older than myself who I looked up to and wanted to respect. But not everything they said was helpful. Here are some examples of 'worldly wisdom' dressed up as spirituality:

- *'We are just unworthy sinners saved by grace.'* No we are not! We are children of God. We are blood bought saints who are indwelt by the Spirit of God, the Spirit of adoption, who tells us we are sons of God, not unworthy worms.
- *'God provides for our needs not our wants.'* No, this is another distortion of God's word. Orphans get their needs met in an orphanage. Prisoners get their needs met in a prison. But God has brought us into his family. He has bestowed covenant blessings upon us and like any good earthly father, he delights to bless his children with more than they simply need.

- *'Don't be greedy, be content with what you have in life.'* Here is another Christian myth. This saying originates from the time when rationing was common, when frugality was seen as a virtue and yes, times were genuinely challenging. True godly contentment is rooted in gratitude and thanksgiving. Alongside this is a godly 'discontentment' that causes us to embrace our God-given dreams and creative gifts for the betterment of ourselves, our families, churches and society as a whole.

I discovered another spiritual law as a young man. God gives even more to those he can trust with what they have been given. 'For to everyone who has, more will be given, and he will have abundance; but from him who does not have, even what he has will be taken away' (Matthew 25:29). When you commit to growing in your faith, that faith attracts more and more to itself. The Christian life is a walk, 'from faith to faith'. Faith will keep on growing because it is a kingdom quality.

Othniel, the first of many

I like to imagine God the father watching these events unfold and taking counsel in the Trinity. 'Look at Othniel, he is the kind of person we can entrust to handle the anointing power that we want to unleash on the earth. He has the character. He has the heart.' When the need arose for a deliverer for God's people the Father and the Son turned to the Holy Spirit and sent him from heaven. The Spirit of God eagerly cooperated and rushed upon Othniel in power. He defeated the enemy and judged the people.

Othniel was a prototype, the first of many to come, an anointed deliverer. He did not emerge from a vacuum. He had the heart of one sold out for God and the interests of his people. He was a man of courage. He also valued inheritance. He had a prosperity mind-set and understood the covenant he was in.

The devil had not witnessed such a thing as the anointing before. He was confused. How does Othniel do this? What is behind it? But things only went from bad to worse. Othniel was followed by a string of other deliverers who inflicted defeat on the enemies of God's people in just the same way as Othniel. What panicked the devil more than anything was that every time the Holy Spirit came upon a man or woman, they became invincible and he was defeated. Every time!

The anointed deliverers always won. They always succeeded. That is the nature of the anointing. The devil was not fighting a human but God himself. So what could he do? At some point in the devilish mind the penny must have dropped and he realised that he was not up against human beings but the Spirit of almighty God himself. As he was no match for the anointing his only course of action was to make a personal attack on the deliverer. From then on, this became the focus of his energy – to discover the secret of how these men attracted the anointing and then rob them of that secret.

This didn't happen immediately. As the book of Judges takes its course there are other people upon whom the Holy Spirit descended and caused them to do great exploits, defeat the enemy and deliver God's people Israel. There was Deborah and Barak. Then we have noted Gideon who defeated the Midianites. Then came Jephthah who defeated the Ammonites East of the river Jordan. Finally we read of Samson. This is where the devil became completely thwarted and frustrated and Satan's quest became especially urgent and for good reason. Samson was born specifically to defeat the Philistines once and for all and he operated in an extraordinary level of the supernatural. But Samson was also deeply flawed and suffered the loss of his anointing. This leads us perfectly into our examination of Samson and why this happened.

6

Why anointed leaders fall

One of the most baffling and upsetting issues we face in the body of Christ is the moral failure of anointed, successful leaders. Every time we hear a leader has fallen or ungodly behaviour has been exposed, it sends shock waves through the church landscape. We feel pain, shame, confusion and perhaps worst of all, we see Christians who are damaged personally, who lose their faith or even turn against the church they once loved.

It raises so many questions. How can a leader operate in an anointing while living in deception, sin or compromise? How could it have continued for so long unchecked? What can we do to prevent or at least minimize this from happening? I have personally witnessed too many wonderful men of God fall in one way or another and conclude that none of us are immune. Those of us who stand must take the greatest of care lest we fall too.

In this chapter I am taking the Life of Samson as an object lesson on this perplexing and distressing subject. He is an extreme example; one of the most anointed of God's servants in the whole Bible while also being one of the most morally flawed. He was called of God, born of God, used by God, failed God and yet restored by God too. So we should be able to learn some things from his life.

Moral failure among anointed leaders tends to fall into one of three categories; sexual misconduct, financial misconduct or ungodly leadership behaviour. This latter one is of itself, the source of a number of issues such as false teaching, abusive behaviour or authoritarian leadership. Samson's issue was his sexual failing and as it happens this is the issue which seems to cause the most damage and attract the most attention in the church today.

Get God's perspective

Samson is a Bible character who receives almost universally bad press. We know of him as 'the man who failed.' Preachers and authors scratch around for any redeeming features with which to salvage something praise-worthy from his life. After all, he squandered his God-given call, he gave in to temptation and he failed his nation. Could it have been any worse? But hold on, there is another side to the story of Samson. Perhaps God viewed him differently? We need to face this possibility before going any further. Allow me to explain.

Apart from the book of Judges, Samson is mentioned only once in all the Scriptures. But the location of that mention is significant. He sits alongside Abraham, Joseph, Moses and David in Hebrews chapter 11, the hall of fame of the heroes of faith. Here is the precise passage:

> *By faith the walls of Jericho fell down after they were encircled for seven days. By faith the harlot Rahab did not perish with those who did not believe, when she had received the spies with peace. And what more shall I say? For the time would fail me to tell of Gideon and Barak and* ***Samson*** *and Jephthah, also of David and Samuel and the prophets: who through faith subdued kingdoms, worked righteousness, obtained promises, stopped the mouths of lions, quenched the violence of fire, escaped the edge of the*

> *sword, out of weakness were made strong, became valiant in battle, turned to flight the armies of the aliens. Women received their dead raised to life again.*
>
> Hebrews 11:30-35

Notice that Samson is not being condemned for his failure but commended for his faith. He has not been placed in Hebrews chapter 11 to serve as a warning for us to avoid but as an example for us to follow. At first glance this seems extraordinary. The only conclusion we can draw from this is that when we see Samson's name in Hebrews 11:32 we are viewing his life from heaven's perspective. We are discovering how God evaluates Samson and this is something very different. In Hebrews 11 God defines his life by his faith not his failing, and in the final analysis God's estimation is the one that matters.

How would you or I comment on Samson if we were writing about him in the New Testament? *'Now let Samson's life be a warning to us all of how badly you can finish if you don't take care.'* But that is not how the New Testament comments on Samson. He is celebrated as a man of faith sitting next to David, Samuel and the prophets! I am not in the least bit excusing the behaviour of flawed leaders or the damage perpetrated by them. I simply want to show that God is still greater than both and the life of Samson demonstrates this.

Faith defined by deeds

Despite his failings, Samson lived a life of faith. He operated in the anointing, defeating God's enemies and judged the people of Israel for 20 years. Even with his failures, the Bible elevates his deeds of faith. This is wonderful and should come first when we consider God's flawed servants today. But more than that, a number of faith descriptions are listed in Hebrews 11 that only really apply to what Samson accomplished in his death, not his life.

- *'Subdued kingdoms'* – he destroyed the Philistines by pulling down their temple
- *'Obtained promises'* – the angel's prophecy to his parents was fulfilled in his death
- *'Out of weakness were made strong'* – his strength was restored for his final deed

In the moment of his death Samson's greatest faith was manifest and his life purpose was fulfilled. If Samson had not come back from failure in the last moments of his life the story would have been very different. But that is not what happened. A very questionable character finished his life in spectacular fashion and his death changed everything. Samson's reputation was tilted by a single act of faith. In other words moral failure does not have to be the end of the road, there is always hope.

Something must have taken place in that Philistine prison for this to be true. God must have been at work in his heart. Samson was not finished with. How do we know Samson's heart had changed? Because when God gave him the opportunity, he was ready to exercise faith and God anointed him again. The months he spent grinding corn in the prison, blinded and humiliated, must have been a period of deep reflection and repentance or he would not have recognised his moment of destiny. During his incarceration he turned from the shame of failure to repentance and readiness. When Samson cried out to God and pushed on those temple pillars, the anointing surged through his body again.

It is incredible to realise that Samson was able to come back from the most brutal failure such that his faith is recorded in the New Testament. However, failure and disqualification are not limited to the few high profile leaders. It could be that you are struggling over an area of failure in your own life. Perhaps you have lost your anointing or been disqualified from ministry.

If so do not allow past failures or lost opportunities keep you from surrendering your life to Christ again. Refuse to live in regret or remorse! Do not keep company with victim identity. Let Samson's finish be an inspiration for you right now to draw a line in the ground and offer yourself unreservedly to God and his purpose.

Seeing from heaven's perspective

Getting God's viewpoint applies to every human life not just Samson because we are all flawed. You don't know the truth about anyone until you know what God has to say about them. We tend to focus on our failures, God focusses on our faith. Failures appear before us like huge red blotches on our life record. Meanwhile God is recording our deeds of faith. Failures seem to possess a life of their own and shout with a voice much louder than they deserve. But making mistakes and failures does not necessarily disqualify you from your destiny. What matters most of all is how you finish. Samson did not end as a failure and even God's wounded warriors have the opportunity to come back and win.

We should be very careful in expressing our opinion about someone else especially when the headline facts seem so clear. Samson's failures invite us to dismiss him yet God recognises him for his faith and only God sees with perfect vision. There is room for only one person on the judgment seat and that is Jesus and guess what, he loves me and died for me on the cross and Jesus died for the one you want to judge and condemn. The way to experience the mercy and grace of God in your life is to show it to yourself and to others and allow Jesus to be the judge.

Let's take David as an example, when Saul tragically lost his life due to his flawed character, David did not rejoice but mourned, celebrated Saul and declared 'Tell it not in Gath, proclaim it not in the streets of Ashkelon' (2 Samuel 1:20). In other words don't magnify the tragedy. Don't amplify the enemy's gloating. Just as with Samson, only God sees the whole picture. It is easy to think we understand a person or a situation when in fact we only have limited knowledge. It is better to keep quiet and pray. Everything I've heard preached about Samson has been negative, but God viewed him differently.

Samson's life is a reminder that it is God who chooses those he uses. There is no perfectly spotless vessel of God. We do not excuse sin, compromise or disobedience but neither do we deny the grace of God on the flawed men and women God has used so powerfully over the centuries. In all my study of the lives of God's generals, I have observed how God displays his goodness through earthen vessels. You and I might not have chosen some of these people but God did.

Samson and Christ the anointed one.

Before we continue I want to share with you the deeper prophetic significance of Samson's life. If you think it crazy that Samson is commended as a man of faith there is more to come. The Philistines thought they had Samson just where they wanted him; blinded, bound and abandoned by his God. But they were wrong. They had no idea how the plan of God was working in this seemingly disastrous situation. Does this sound familiar? It should because Samson's life speaks of Christ.

Samson is a type or shadow of Christ, the anointed one himself. You may find it shocking to even conceive that our wonderful saviour could in any way be a compared to such a character as Samson. But it is true, in fact Samson's life and especially his death, fore-shadow the life and death of Christ. Samson was stretched between two pillars, bound, mocked and seemingly defeated by the enemy. But in one moment of self-sacrifice, everything changed and a ruthless enemy was soundly defeated – a picture of Christ!

Like Christ, Samson was chosen before his birth for a divine purpose. Other judges were anointed by the Spirit, only Samson was chosen and anointed by the Spirit to bring complete deliverance to God's people. Unlike Christ Samson failed to live up to his calling in his life but just like Christ, he did so in his death. But there are more prophetic parallels linking Samson and Christ, not just his mission to destroy God's enemy.

- Samson was a Nazarite from birth – just like Jesus

Notice how the angel of God announced the birth of Samson to his mother:

> *For behold, you shall conceive and bear a son. And no razor shall come upon his head, for the child shall be a Nazirite to God from the womb; and he shall begin to deliver Israel out of the hand of the Philistines.*
>
> Judges 13:5

Samson was separated to God from his birth, so was Jesus. At his birth the angels announced to the shepherds the purpose for which he was born – 'the saviour who is Christ the Lord'. Furthermore Jesus was from Nazareth (Matthew 2:23). The name 'Nazareth' means consecrated, crowned or separated. We will see the significance of this soon.

- Samson's birth was announced by angels – just like Jesus

> *And the Angel of the LORD appeared to the woman and said to her, "Indeed now, you are barren and have*

> *borne no children, but you shall conceive and bear a son. Now therefore, please be careful not to drink wine or similar drink, and not to eat anything unclean".*
>
> Judges 13:3-4

Samson's father Manoah and his wife were childless. But an angel of God visited Manoah's wife with a message that echoes the one given to Mary the mother of Jesus.

- Samson was conceived through the work of the Holy Spirit – just like Jesus

Samson's mother couldn't conceive naturally but God opened her womb. Mary's conception of the baby Jesus was by direct intervention of the Holy Spirit.

- Samson ministered in the power of the Spirit – just like Jesus

It would seem that Samson was endowed with an anointing of the Spirit from an early age. The Spirit was stirring him and he was aware of his call to defeat Israel's enemy the Philistines. So just as with Jesus, Samson operated in a supernatural ministry.

- Not only his birth and life, but even more so, Samson's death is laden with prophetic parallels to Christ. Indeed Samson's death at the hands of the Philistines represents a vivid portrayal of Christ's death.
- He was publically mocked and humiliated, just as Jesus was. Both kept silent before their accusers, trusting God in the face of the enemy.
- He died while stretched out in the physical shape of the cross. What a powerful picture of the death

of Christ. He stood with his arms out, at his place of death just like Jesus.

- His death was vicarious – he sacrificed his life to save God's people. Jesus's victory was the same, he stood in our place as our substitute so we could be delivered.
- He killed more in his death than in his life. Jesus did many mighty works in his life but his greatest victory was in his death when Satan was conquered once and for all.

So not only was God pleased to commend Samson as a man of faith, he chose him to speak of his Son, to hint at how the messiah would give his life to deliver his people from sin and Satan. Now we are going to discover the greatest reason why anointed people fall and what we can do to protect the anointing in our lives.

The secret of Samson's strength

The devil learned through the lives of the Judges that the greatest threat to his activity was the anointing. I like to imagine Satan trying to figure out what to do with those anointed deliverers like Othniel and Gideon and feeling thwarted time and again. But then matters got worse with the arrival of Samson who posed a threat to his activities like no other. Samson had a unique call to utterly defeat the Philistines. Hence the urgency to destroy this person who carried the anointing and therefore the question, 'What is the secret of your great strength' (Judges 16:6). The devil was about to go on the offensive.

The source of Samson's strength was of course the Holy Spirit. But at a deeper level, the secret of Samson's anointing was his separation to God. Samson was a Nazarite from birth. What the devil learned is that although you can't attack the anointing you can attack the person who carries the anointing when they step out of their separation to God. Here is the lesson we must learn:

The first key to receiving and sustaining an anointed life is your separation to God!

The secret of Samson's strength lay in his ability to protect the anointing through consecration. This is supremely important. From the time the devil discovered this secret it was a secret no longer. Once the devil discovered the secret to Samson's anointing he could apply what he knew to every man or woman of God who was anointed as Samson was.

> *And He said to me, 'Behold, you shall conceive and bear a son. Now drink no wine or similar drink, nor eat anything unclean, for the child shall be a Nazirite to God from the womb to the day of his death.'*
>
> Judges 13:7

That is how it remains to this day. The devil cannot destroy the anointing because he is up against God but he will do everything to attack the anointed man or woman. His methods of attack may constantly change. The means by which the devil coaxes men and women out of their separation differ according to the individual concerned. We see the issue for Samson. But what else might it be: worry, distraction, offence, busyness, jealousy, greed, pride, entitlement, vanity, error, deception? Satan will target the anointed child of God doing everything he can if possible to wear them down and defeat them.

I have observed this over and over throughout my life – how Satan has exploited character weakness to disqualify anointed men and women. It is heart-breaking but terribly predictable. The same old tactics again and again; sexual failure, financial failure or carnal behaviour. Satan wormed his way in at the point of vulnerability and that wonderful anointing was nullified. The devil seeks to shift us from our place of separation because then we will be weakened and become like anyone else. The hour we live in is dark and the global church faces unprecedented threats. It is therefore absolutely vital that we remain and abide in the anointing of God's Spirit at all times. Benny Hinn has championed the anointing for decades like few others and yet has shared more recently how he came close to losing his way because of compromising his separation to God. In his book 'The Anointing' he says, 'Start seeking God. Pay the price. Turn your life right side up, and he will anoint your head clear down to your feet'.[2] The anointing is our greatest weapon and the thing we must guard at all cost.

Samson had a weakness for women. He constantly flirted and bent the rules in order to satisfy his wandering eye. Someone other than the Philistines was watching this behaviour. Even though God continued to use him it was just a matter of time before Samson's compromise would catch up with him and cost him his anointing.

First in Judges 14 we read that he married a Philistine woman from a place called Timnah. That got messy and complicated. Then in Judges 16 we read he had a relationship with a Philistine prostitute from the city of Gaza. That didn't end well either! All this time he continued to operate in a life of faith and the anointing of the Spirit of God. It is the same contradiction we see in God's fallen servants today. Sometimes

---

2. Benny Hinn, The Anointing, Destiny Image, page 47

there is a long period of successful ministry before their flaws catch up with them and they are taken out of ministry. Samson's final downfall was at the hands of Delilah and it was while sleeping on her lap that he experienced defeat.

> *Then she said to him, "How can you say, 'I love you,' when your heart is not with me? You have mocked me these three times, and have not told me where your great strength lies." And it came to pass, when she pestered him daily with her words and pressed him, so that his soul was vexed to death, that he told her all his heart, and said to her, "No razor has ever come upon my head, for I have been a Nazirite to God from my mother's womb. If I am shaven, then my strength will leave me, and I shall become weak, and be like any other man."*
>
> *When Delilah saw that he had told her all his heart, she sent and called for the lords of the Philistines, saying, "Come up once more, for he has told me all his heart." So the lords of the Philistines came up to her and brought the money in their hand. Then she lulled him to sleep on her knees, and called for a man and had him shave off the seven locks of his head. Then she began to torment him, and his strength left him. And she said, "The Philistines are upon you, Samson!" So he awoke from his sleep, and said, "I will go out as before, at other times, and shake myself free!" But he did not know that the LORD had departed from him.*
>
> Judges 16:15-20

When Delilah wore Samson down, pleading with him day after day, he rolled over, confessed the secret of his separation and was snared. When the Philistines rushed upon Samson, he had no strength in him. He was bound, blinded and put in the prison to grind corn. This once great man was humiliated because he compromised his separation to God at his point of weakness.

Nazareth – the power of separation

Now we are going to dig deeper into the power of separation to God. This was the secret of Samson's anointing. It was the secret of Christ's anointing and it is your secret and my secret too.

When we look into the New Testament we observe that Christ dwelt in Nazareth, Matthew records that it was said of Jesus, 'He shall be called a Nazarene' (Matthew 2:23). We therefore have to conclude that somewhere in the Old Covenant this is stated. But where does the law or the prophets actually say that the Christ will be called a Nazarene? The only place you will find this expression is in the story of Samson; Judges 13:5 says, 'He shall be called a Nazarite'.[3]

The name 'Nazareth' means separated, crowned, consecrated or sanctified. It comes from a root Hebrew word *netzer* which means a branch, the place where a tree separates. So Jesus, the anointed one, came from Nazareth, a city whose name means 'separation'. So when we read, 'Christ comes from Nazareth', it literally translates, **'the anointing comes from separation'**. What clearer message could we ask for! The source of the anointing is separation to God.

When Peter stood before the crippled beggar he said, 'Silver and gold I do not have, but what I do have I give you: In the

---

3. It is also true that Isaiah 11:1 states, *'There shall come forth a Rod from Jesse, and a branch shall grow out of his roots'.* The word 'branch' is a translation of the Hebrew *netzer*, a place where a branch separates into two. The word 'Nazarene' can also be derived from *netzer*.

name of **Jesus Christ of Nazareth**, rise up and walk' (Acts 3:6). The anointing of Christ the one who separated himself to God, rushed through Peter's hands and the crippled man was healed. That same anointing flows today through all who have separated themselves to God.

In John chapter one we have a further insight into the priority and power of separation. Satan will do anything possible to keep us from living a consecrated life because that is the source of the anointing. Look carefully at the following passage from John's gospel:

> *The following day Jesus wanted to go to Galilee, and He found Philip and said to him, "Follow me." Now Philip was from Bethsaida, the city of Andrew and Peter. Philip found Nathanael and said to him, "We have found Him of whom Moses in the law, and also the prophets, wrote – Jesus of Nazareth, the son of Joseph." And Nathanael said to him, "Can anything good come out of Nazareth?" Philip said to him, "Come and see." Jesus saw Nathanael coming toward Him, and said of him, "Behold, an Israelite indeed, in whom is no deceit!" Nathanael said to Him, "How do you know me?" Jesus answered and said to him, "Before Philip called you, when you were under the fig tree, I saw you." Nathanael answered and said to Him, "Rabbi, You are the Son of God! You are the King of Israel!" Jesus answered and said to him, "Because I said to you, 'I saw you under the fig tree,' do you believe? You will see greater things than these." And He said to him, "Most assuredly, I say to you, hereafter you shall see heaven open, and the angels of God ascending and descending upon the Son of Man."*
>
> John 1:43-51

Nathaniel said of Jesus, 'Can anything good come out of Nazareth' (John 1:45-47). What is really being said here? It was of course a slur. It was an insult. But look deeper with me. Nazareth means separation. So this slur literally translates, 'Can anything good come from separation to God?' The fact is that Christ the anointed one came out of Nazareth. What could be more powerful and prophetic than that! But the devil seeks to undermine the power of consecration. He is in effect saying: *'What good can come from your separation to God?' 'What possible benefit can there be in all that devotion and consecration to the Lord?' 'What value has it been for you up until now?*

Separation to God is the first principle to experiencing his anointing. 'The Christ comes from Nazareth.' The anointing comes from separation. It is better to go to glory seeking for more of God than idling your time way. Jesus' life was marked by separation to his father. And when the time came, he went into the Jordan to be baptized by John – a supreme act of separation – and at the point in time the Holy Spirit descended on him and his ministry of power began. Do all you can to follow his example and refuse to back down – ever! God has not finished with you yet. Make this the point in time when you turn your heart back to God and renew your separation to him that he might use you as never before to his glory.

You may even have fallen into some kind of sin like other servants of God and concluded he can't use you any longer. You may have become discouraged for lack of evidence of the anointing in your life. You may have become distracted by other priorities and relegated the anointing. Resist the temptation to devalue the place of devotion. Refuse to compromise your consecration! Do not be discouraged. Shut out the cynical voice of the enemy. The unchanging truth is that the anointing comes from consecration! This is the path to the anointing. Protect it. Value it. Prize it.

Isolated or accountable

I want to finish this chapter with one more important observation about Samson that is relevant to protecting the anointing. There is no evidence that Samson had anyone in his life who could challenge his behaviour and help him protect his calling. We do know this is not the case with other leaders in the Old Testament.

- Barak had Deborah the prophet to challenge him to overcome his fear and lead Israel to victory over their enemies.
- King Saul had the prophet Samuel in his life to challenge him over his pride and disobedience.
- King David had Nathan the prophet in his court who challenged him over his adultery with Bathsheba and murder of Uriah, Bathsheba's husband.

It is interesting to note that in each case it was a prophet who brought the accountability. In fact in the Bible it is prophets more than anyone else that we find challenging sinful behaviour and calling people back to God. When we arrive in the New Testament, we see an abundance of examples of the early church operating in accountable relationships. In fact the majority of the New Testament letters are corrective appeals to churches and leaders. This should be no surprise as the church is a community of God's people, living stones being built together in honest and transparent relationships.

Samson however, had no one. Even though the prophet Samuel straddled the time of the judges and the kings and was a contemporary of Samson's, there is no mention of any relationship or interaction between the two. Why could Samuel not have been a voice to Samson? We don't know but the lesson is plain to see. Samson was an isolated man and therefore vulnerable to falling.

> *Two are better than one, because they have a good reward for their labor. For if they fall, one will lift up his companion. But woe to him who is alone when he falls, for he has no one to help him up.*
>
> Ecclesiastes 4:9-10

We should make sure we have people in our lives who are prepared to challenge us and turn a few stones if necessary – and not simply friends or familiar colleagues, but as we have seen, the voice of those who hear from God, whether they are recognised as prophets as such or not.

For accountability to work effectively, you cannot be passive, you have to hold yourself to account and that requires humility. It is possible to have the right people around you but if you simply maintain a distance from them, questionable behaviour can continue undetected. You can be busy, active in church and surrounded by people but withdrawn from them on the inside. Isolation is not simply physical distance, it is internal disconnection too.

But secondly those to whom you claim to be accountable must be the kind of people who can take initiative in your life. In the words of the management tutorials, 'You can only expect what you inspect'. What is at stake is the operation of the anointing manifest in you and me to a needy world. The devil will do anything he can to neutralize God's anointed people, let's do everything we can to protect ourselves from that ever happening. The lesson is simple for everyone, for ourselves and anointed leaders everywhere. To protect the anointing on our lives, we have to guard our connection to the Holy Spirit and our connection to trusted spiritual authority.

7

The Secret Place

After pastoring our first church for nearly 10 years my wife and I planted LifeSpring Church and LifeSpring Ministries in 1998. The first few years were a whirlwind of activity and blessing. The church was soon rooted and the future looked certain, or so we thought. By the year 2006 however, it felt as though we had hit a ceiling. We were tired, we needed help in our marriage and we faced some pastoral issues that we did not have the tools to tackle. Our own hearts needed healing and restoring. We desperately needed a breakthrough. So we made the courageous decision to pull back from much of our activity and reposition ourselves to hear God and experience whatever he had for us.

It was at this time and as part of this process, the Lord began challenging me about the importance of the anointing and how to walk in unbroken intimacy with the Holy Spirit. He led me to study the life of one of God's most remarkable servants, Smith Wigglesworth. I had previously read a number of books about this extraordinary man so I scanned my shelves afresh, tracked down every one of them and began digging in. I was looking for the keys to his anointed life and in the process of time I believe I found three; here they are.

- Wigglesworth had a relationship with God's Word

Most of us read the Word of God, some of us perhaps read and study it more consistently, Wigglesworth took things a step further; he developed a relationship with God's Word. It never left his side. He took a New Testament with him everywhere. His friend and biographer Albert Hibbert, recorded that the Bible was the only book Wigglesworth read and that he never went longer than 15 minutes without reading it. Whenever he received guests into his home he would inevitably be reading the Scriptures to them within the hour! From there it would lead to a prayer time and finally to a hearty meal prepared by his daughter in law.

Wigglesworth immersed himself in the truths of God's Word to the degree that he became one with the Word. He was an extension of the Word. The gap between what the Word of God declares and what we experience is one of the greatest barriers to experiencing the supernatural. That gap was a hair breadth in the life of this man of God. The result was a highly developed gift of faith. The Word of God, the source of faith, was like a reservoir within him from which he could draw supernatural resources at any time. As a consequence he walked in an unwavering trust in everything God said in his Word and remarkable results followed.

- Wigglesworth walked in love

There is no doubt Wigglesworth could be outspoken and intolerant. This caused people to divide in their opinion of him. Furthermore some of his dealings with needy people were unconventional even at times to the point of being controversial. As a result, incidents became exaggerated, testimonies embellished and some of the exceptional healing stories recounted as if they were normal. All of this is unfortunate because under the skin of this blunt Yorkshireman beat a very compassionate heart. He would devote hours to praying for someone in private in order to get a breakthrough for them. Sometimes he took long train journeys just to visit one person in need. He would weep easily and listen intently in the presence of the sick and suffering.

Wigglesworth was motivated by the love of God – pure and simple. He did not seek the spectacular or need the crowds that flocked to hear him preach. It was the love of God that moved him and he followed the impulses of his heart in helping people wherever he could. It was this compassion that formed a channel for God's power to flow easily through him just like Jesus when confronted with the leper in Mark's gospel.

> *Now a leper came to Him, imploring Him, kneeling down to Him and saying to Him, "If you are willing, you can make me clean." Then Jesus, moved with compassion, stretched out His hand and touched him, and said to him, "I am willing; be cleansed." As soon as He had spoken, immediately the leprosy left him, and he was cleansed.*
>
> Mark 1:40-42

The power of God flowed through the compassionate heart of Jesus to the needy and healed him. The same was true of Smith Wigglesworth. Albert Hibbert explains: 'Often people have asked me what I consider to be the secret of Wigglesworth's power. There were several aspects. One secret was his love and compassion for those in need.'[4]

- Wigglesworth enjoyed intimate fellowship with the Holy Spirit

It is here that we reach the central issue in the life of Smith Wigglesworth. He developed a fellowship with the person of

---

4. Albert Hibbert, Smith Wigglesworth, the Secret of his Power, page 40

the Holy Spirit himself, paying very careful attention to listen to him and obey whatever he said. Wigglesworth considered this to be the greatest form of prayer, the moment by moment communion with the Spirit of God.

Sometimes he would hear the Holy Spirit so clearly and step out in his instruction. He would not flinch, however strange the instruction might be, but time and again God came through in power, the sick were healed and the dead were raised. In his biography of Wigglesworth, Stanley Howard Frodsham shares what is perhaps one of the most profound insights of his life. I am going to quote this at length so you catch the full impact of what is said.

> *He (Wigglesworth) became acquainted with a very godly minister who was one time visiting England and who carried with him an unusual degree of the presence of God. His preaching was plain and unadorned, but he took his hearers into conscious contact with the Lord. Many zealous souls sought to learn the secret of his power, but he was reluctant to tell them. However, after he had prayed about the matter, the Lord gave him liberty to tell those who inquired the secret of his deep spiritual ministry. He said, 'Years ago the Spirit of God began to speak to me, but I was too busy to heed his voice. He persisted until I commenced to go aside when he spoke so that I could hear what God the Lord had to say. This became my manner of life. I obeyed his pleading voice until now at the slightest breath of the Spirit, I leave everyone and everything to be in his presence, to hear and obey his word.'*[5]

5. Stanley Howard Frodsham, Smith Wigglesworth, Apostle of Faith, page 75

The secret place is the open secret to living in the anointing of the Holy Spirit. If you are hungry for more than a fleeting experience of the Holy Spirit, if you want to sustain his power and live in his authority – then cultivate the secret place in your own life. Discover practically what that looks like. Devote yourself to Him every day, pay the price and never, ever give up! The secret place is a vital living connection with the Holy Spirit. This is not just theory but part of our very personal journey of discovery. I am going to explain. My journey of discovery not only took me into the lives of some of God's great Generals, it took me to several Bible passages where the Holy Spirit shone his light and gave me living revelation into this life in the Holy Spirit.

Manner and mission

Let's begin by going back to the person of Samson. It was here that God spoke to me with a word that was to prove life-changing. I was reading in the Book of Judges chapter 13 from the English Standard Version of the Bible. It is the story of how Samson's mother and father received the promise of a son. They were childless but the angel of God appeared to Samson's mother and announced the birth of a very special boy. The husband Manoah, was not present at the time. A while later the angel of God appeared again to Manoah's wife while she was in the field. This time a servant was able to call Manoah and he came running to speak to the angel.

> *And Manoah arose and went after his wife and came to the man and said to him, "Are you the man who spoke to this woman?" And he said, "I am." And Manoah said, "Now when your words come true, what is to be the child's manner of life, and what is his mission?"*
>
> Judges 13:11-12

We have already taken a deep dive into the life of Samson in an earlier chapter, but I want to share another very personal lesson from the story right here in the announcement of his birth. Do you notice the question Manoah asked the angel; 'What is to be the child's manner of life, and what is his mission?' The words leapt off the page and hit my heart. Samson was to be defined by these two things, his manner of life and his mission in life. His mission in life was to destroy God's enemies the Philistines and judge his people Israel. His manner of life was his separation to God's presence represented in his Nazarite vows.

I realised that Samson did not lose his anointing because he forgot his mission in life. Far from it, he was constantly attacking and defeating the Philistines. Samson's issue was that he let go of his manner of life. He despised his separation to God and the presence of God left him as a consequence. To quote the Bible at the tragic moment in Samson's life, '. . . he did not know that the LORD had departed from him' (Judges 16:20). The gifts and calling of God are irrevocable (Romans 11:29), not so the anointing, God can withdraw it from us. On that day Samson discovered this truth for himself.

I heard the voice of God, it was clear and simple, 'Make my presence your manner of life'. Let me explain, I already loved and valued the presence of God. But like any serious hard working pastor, I was also highly goal orientated and purpose driven. I derived a huge amount of fulfilment from what I achieved in life. In addition I did what most of us do when we hit a challenge – dig in deeper, pray harder and press on. Don't misunderstand me, ministry is hard work. But just like the power steering of an automobile, we don't fool ourselves that when we work at the wheel, the power is coming from our own effort. It is the car engine that is supplying the power! So too in ministry, we are instruments in God's hand. The power comes from him.

I responded to God's word immediately by focusing on spending priority time in the presence of the Lord on a daily basis. It was an opportunity to put ministry priorities aside for a concentrated season in order to recalibrate my heart and create a place where God could speak. The mornings became my time apart and this continued on a daily basis for several months. I also began studying what the Bible had to say about this concept of the secret place. Finally, my wife Ursula and I determined we would go the whole distance with whatever the Lord wanted to say and do in our lives.

During this time I came to realise that my goal-focused life was due to more than personality or priorities – it was all about the heart. From childhood I had always derived value and meaning from the things I accomplished. When I came to Christ I carried this value system with me and ultimately into my ministry. I was driven by the need to achieve ministry goals. It was classic orphan-heartedness. In the words of Joyce Meyer I was suffering from an 'approval deficit'. Instead of living *from* a place of approval in my heavenly father's love for me, I was living *for* his approval based on what I was doing for him. The Lord kept revealing more. I read Mark's account of how Jesus chose his disciples:

> *And He went up on the mountain and called to Him those He Himself wanted. And they came to Him. Then He appointed twelve, that they might be with Him and that He might send them out to preach, and to have power to heal sicknesses and to cast out demons.*
>
> Mark 3:13-15

Do you see the order; Jesus chose his closest ministers first of all to be with him! Then from that place they were to work for him. Their mission of life followed their manner of life.

The success of the disciples' ministry would spring from their relationship with Jesus. He was their constant companion. They were his friends and disciples; they walked, talked, lived and learned from him all the time.

God is interested in both our manner of life and our mission in life. Our mission represents the fulfilment of God's purpose in the earth. It is absolutely vital. Our manner of life represents our intimate connection with the Holy Spirit. A manner of life without a mission renders us fruitless and irrelevant. I have witnessed plenty of people who value intimacy with the Lord but strangely it doesn't lead them into bearing fruit for him. I have seen churches that devoted themselves to seeking more of the Holy Spirit and yet ironically shrivel away because there is no outlet for all they are receiving.

On the other hand a mission in life without a manner of life cannot be sustained either. Mission is essential and mission will involve work and energy. But we must understand that Jesus did not say fruit comes by working harder but abiding deeper. The works that give God the most glory are those that emanate from intimacy with him.

Shared life

> *The grace of the Lord Jesus Christ, and the love of God, and the communion of the Holy Spirit be with you all. Amen.*
>
> 2 Corinthians 13:14

For the most part we have missed the power of these words of the apostle Paul because they have been relegated to a blessing at meals times or a benediction at the end of a religious service. But Paul is expressing in the strongest terms, his desire that the Corinthian believers would have a deeper personal encounter with each member of the Trinity; Father, Son and Holy Spirit. Each person of the Godhead carries a particular experience of God to us as human beings and we see this in many passages of the New Testament. This is how it works:

- The love of God is particularly associated with the Father because God's love is a father's love. 'Behold what manner of love the Father has bestowed on us, that we should be called children of God . . .' (1 John 3:1). The love of God our heavenly Father is an experience to be enjoyed.
- Grace is found in Jesus Christ. 'For you know the grace of our Lord Jesus Christ . . .' (2 Corinthians 8:9). The love of God is demonstrated in the grace of Jesus Christ. It is unmerited and undeserved, our position in Christ and his privilege and power.
- Intimacy is connected with The Holy Spirit. Paul uses the expression, '. . . the fellowship of the Holy Spirit . . .' (2 Corinthians 13:14 ESV). The Holy Spirit is the person of the Trinity who comes into our hearts to bring the goodness of God into our lives.

This word 'fellowship' or 'communion' is the Greek word *koinonia* which is best translated 'partnership' or 'shared life'. It describes an intimate connection between ourselves and the Holy Spirit. It is where two distinct lives are joined so closely they are indivisible. That defines the goal of the Holy Spirit in your life and mine, he wants intimate connection. This is what Adam experienced originally in the garden with God, what he lost in the fall and what God makes available to us again in Christ.

One of the most widespread and fascinating plant organisms in existence is lichen. There are around 20,000 species of lichen covering 6-8 percent of the earth's surface – more than the rain forests! These tiny organisms live on rocks, trees, plants and even houses. We have been aware of their existence of course for thousands of years but it was not until the 1970's that it was discovered that lichen is in fact not one but two separate organisms, a fungi and an algae (or bacteria), living as one. The fungi acts as a host for the algae to live and the algae provides an external source of sugar on which the fungi depends.

Lichen, one of creation's wonders and a picture of the believer's relationship with the Holy Spirit

It is a beautiful illustration of the partnership or shared life we enjoy with the third person of the Trinity. The human heart was designed to be the perfect home for the Holy Spirit, we are his temple. The dwelling place of God is men and women. But he in turn provides life and energy to us. He vitalizes us at the new birth and abides in us from that time. That is a picture of *koinonia* – the closest relationship possible. The only issue is whether we are consciously cultivating and enjoying that intimacy or not.

The reality of the secret place runs throughout Scripture. It is a place of fellowship around the throne of God, a place where God communes and shares secrets with those who draw near, wait and listen. It is a place where men and women of God have learned to stand in his presence. Psalm 91 is a powerful description of the Secret Place. I encourage you to stop and read it all through. Here are the first two verses:

> *He who dwells in the secret place of the Most High Shall abide under the shadow of the Almighty. I will say of the LORD, "He is my refuge and my fortress; My God, in Him I will trust."*
>
> Psalms 91:1-2

The Hebrew word for 'secret place' in this passage is *sayther*, and it means 'covering, 'hiding' and 'protection'. The word for Most High is *elyon* and the word for Almighty is *el-shaddai*. The secret place is a place of refuge and shelter for the believer. Our protection comes from here. Psalm 91 is incredible. Just look at these further verses for example:

> *Because you have made the LORD your dwelling place the Most High, who is my refuge no evil shall be allowed to befall you, no plague come near your tent.*
>
> Psalm 91:9-10

> *Because he holds fast to me in love, I will deliver him; I will protect him, because he knows my name. When he calls to me, I will answer him; I will be with him in trouble; I will rescue him and honor*

> *him. With long life I will satisfy him and show him my salvation.*
>
> Psalm 91:14-16

This Psalm is frequently used as a source of comfort for believers who are struggling with overwhelming challenges. They turn here for strength; they claim God's promise, and that is absolutely fine. But there are conditions to fulfil. The protection and victory that people seek is dependent on hiding in the secret place! Religiously claiming a promise when you have not fulfilled the conditions is futile. The point is this; if you want the Lord to be your 'el-shaddai', you have to make him your 'most high'.

In the secret place fear is demolished. It is a place of freedom from depression and anxiety. When you know that underneath you are his everlasting arms, that he goes before you and forms your rear guard – you will experience his supernatural peace. No wonder Paul calls it a peace that passes understanding (Philippians 4:7) because it makes no human sense. When circumstances and voices threaten and alarm, you are kept in perfect peace because you are hiding in the secret place of the Most High.

The council of God

> *The secret of the LORD is with those who fear Him,*
> *And He will show them His covenant.*
>
> Psalms 25:14

The Hebrew word for 'secret' in this verse is *sode*; it means intimacy, a sitting, a consultation, a council. The ESV translates this as 'the friendship of the Lord'. It refers to relationship with a familiar acquaintance. It comes from a root word meaning couch, pillow or cushion. *Sode* always refers to an intimate gathering of some kind or another. The same word is used in Job 19:19 where Job speaks of 'intimate friends'.

We can conclude that God has a council! He has an intimate place around his throne that some are evidently enjoying more than others. With these friends he shares his secrets. Those who are listening and available find themselves called upon for special tasks. God loves us equally but not everyone is experiencing his love and intimacy to the same degree.

I will never forget hearing Reinhard Bonnke describe how God asked him to spearhead the 'Minus to Plus' evangelism initiative in the UK in the 1990's. It involved distributing millions of special evangelistic booklets to homes across the country. He initially questioned the Lord about this. After all, he was a crusade evangelist not a literature distributor! This was not his call. He was shocked by what the Holy Spirit said. 'You were not my first choice but my third. I asked two others to do this but they refused!' You see, Reinhard Bonnke was chosen simply because he was willing and available. He was part of the Lord's council chamber and when God needed someone, he used one of those who were hanging around his throne.

This council of the Lord is limited in its scope. It is for those who will pay the price to prioritize His presence. Are you hungry for that? It is a completely different matter to that of coming to the throne for what you need and want. It is about enjoying his presence and listening for whatever he might have on *his* heart to share with those who are there to hear. It is about being more concerned for God's agenda than our own. Are you ready for that adventure?

The Lord is my Shepherd

The final passage of Scripture that become very important to me at this time was Psalm 23. We are so familiar with this

Psalm, but as I meditated on these well-known words of King David, revelation broke over me in wave after wave. The climax of this Psalm is the anointing. As we approach the end, David declares, 'You anoint my head with oil'. But it doesn't begin that way. The lessons of the psalm are meant to equip and prepare us to live an anointed life. They are priceless. What are they? Essentially they are lessons in how to abide in and live from the Secret Place from where the anointing is nurtured.

But first we must understand when exactly David wrote this Psalm, it is eye opening! You may have a mental picture of David sitting on a hillside, in the shade of a tree, with his harp in hand, looking over his sheep as they graze in front of him and into his mind come the words 'The Lord is my shepherd'. The setting of this Psalm is the exact opposite. It was written in one of David's most terrifying moments in life – his escape from Jerusalem as his own son Absalom arrived, leading a mutinous army.

I want you to picture the scene. Absalom's heart had been crushed by the way his sister Tamar had been physically violated by his half-brother Amnon. But worse than that, he was frustrated by the lenient way his father David had dealt with Amnon. Absalom was hurt and angry; the seeds of rebellion were now germinating within him. Absalom took matters into his own hand, killed Amnon and fled to the king of Geshur the Philistine, where he stayed in self-imposed exile for three years.

A peace of kinds was brokered by Joab, David's army chief, and Absalom was able to return to Jerusalem. But David refused to speak to him or even to see him, thus deepening the resentment toward his father. The gulf between them was unbridgeable. Eventually Joab brought father and son together in a surface reconciliation but we can see how deep the enmity had gone in what followed.

> *Now Absalom would rise early and stand beside the way to the gate. So it was, whenever anyone who had a lawsuit came to the king for a decision, that Absalom would call to him and say, "What city are you from?" And he would say, "Your servant is from such and such a tribe of Israel." Then Absalom would say to him, "Look, your case is good and right; but there is no deputy of the king to hear you." Moreover Absalom would say, "Oh, that I were made judge in the land, and everyone who has any suit or cause would come to me; then I would give him justice." And so it was, whenever anyone came near to bow down to him, that he would put out his hand and take him and kiss him. In this manner Absalom acted toward all Israel who came to the king for judgment. So Absalom stole the hearts of the men of Israel.*
>
> 2 Samuel 15:2-6

Absalom stole the hearts of the people of Israel! The conspiracy had begun and within two years had grown to the point that his supporters proclaimed him as king and full scale civil war resulted.

> *Now a messenger came to David, saying, "The hearts of the men of Israel are with Absalom." So David said to all his servants who were with him at Jerusalem, "Arise, and let us flee, or we shall not escape from Absalom. Make haste to depart, lest he overtake us suddenly and bring disaster upon us, and strike the city with the edge of the sword." And the king's servants said to the king, "We are your servants, ready to do whatever my lord the king commands."*
>
> 2 Samuel 15:13-15

David and his retinue of supporters and servants were forced to make a desperate and humiliating escape from his own son, fleeing the city named after him, Jerusalem, the city of David. While Absalom and his forces entered the city, David had already marched some 70 miles through the night, crossing the Jordan River and into the territory of Gilead. Believe it or not, this is the setting for Psalm 23. As David approaches the town of Mahanaim, with his exhausted people, he is met by friends.

> *Now it happened, when David had come to Mahanaim, that Shobi the son of Nahash from Rabbah of the people of Ammon, Machir the son of Ammiel from Lo Debar, and Barzillai the Gileadite from Rogelim, brought beds and basins, earthen vessels and wheat, barley and flour, parched grain and beans, lentils and parched seeds, honey and curds, sheep and cheese of the herd, for David and the people who were with him to eat. For they said, "The people are hungry and weary and thirsty in the wilderness."*
>
> 2 Samuel 17:27-29

At the lowest, most desperate time in his life, God proved to be David's shepherd. He was met with supernatural provision, protection and encouragement. No wonder he wrote these words.

> *The LORD is my shepherd; I shall not want. He makes me to lie down in green pastures; He leads me beside the still waters. He restores my soul.*
>
> Psalms 23:2-3

The way the Psalm begins in Hebrew is with a statement, YHWH-ROHI, literally 'I AM your shepherd'. It is one of

God's covenant names. The eternal 'I AM' is our shepherd. He feeds, he guides, he protects. Before anything else, above any other priority, our Shepherd God invites us to his meadow; to lie down and receive, to feed and to drink – all of which results in him restoring our soul. To successfully walk in paths of righteousness, to navigate dark valleys and to face enemy forces we need to be strong in soul and spirit. A manner of life precedes a mission in life. 'Being' in the secret place comes before 'doing' in the public place.

> *He leads me in the paths of righteousness for His name's sake.*
>
> Psalms 23:3

Those who have cultivated a life of intimacy experience the goodness of God in their everyday life. They learn how to walk in paths of righteousness.

> *Yea, though I walk through the valley of the shadow of death, I will fear no evil; for you are with me; your rod and your staff, they comfort me.*
>
> Psalms 23:4

David wrote these words while he literally faced death in the face. He was walking that valley along with all he loved. And yet in this bleak moment he could declare that God was more than enough. His presence was his companion. Do you see how important it is to cultivate the secret place – it becomes your refuge in the toughest of times.

> *You prepare a table before me in the presence of my enemies; you anoint my head with oil; my cup runs over. Surely goodness and mercy shall follow me all*

the days of my life; and I will dwell in the house of the LORD Forever.

Psalms 23:5-6

Intimacy is more than a prayer retreat or a time of silent meditation. It is experiencing his powerful peace in the most challenging situation. It is the peace of God that passes understanding. Even more profound is the fact that the anointing of the Holy Spirit is not denied us in these extreme times of testing. David says, 'you anoint my head with oil', and that is in the presence of his enemies.

I hope your heart has been stirred by this chapter. My prayer is that you will commit to cultivating a life of intimacy and fellowship, lived in the Secret Place of the Most-High God. Someone once said, 'We can miss the supernatural by looking for the spectacular'. The Secret Place is supernatural. That is where it begins in your life and flows out from there in demonstrations of the Spirit's anointing with power.

8

Learning the ways of the Holy Spirit

Some years ago I was conducting a series of evangelistic healing meetings in North East India. Each night I spoke to those who gathered in an open air arena but what I didn't know until I arrived in the city was that the organizing team had arranged for the meetings to be broadcast live on local TV. So although there were several thousand present in the meetings, there was potentially half a million people being reached in their homes. In addition the team set up a hotline so people could call or text in with messages, testimonies and prayer requests.

The first night I preached a straight forward gospel message and many responded for salvation both in the arena and in their homes. The second night I planned to preach on the subject of divine healing. As I prayed in my hotel room that day I felt the Lord challenge me to minister healing to people in their homes by speaking to them directly into the camera. I had led people in the prayer for salvation in this way the previous night so why not healing too? I accepted the challenge.

So after teaching on divine healing, I prayed for the sick in the venue with wonderful results. Then I declared the same healing power of Jesus to those watching at home. It was amazing to see the hotline immediately light up with people calling to testify to their healing. One outstanding testimony came from a young lady who lay paralyzed in bed, but when I prophesied healing, the power of God hit her and she got up completely healed.

I remember lying on my bed that night thinking about this administration of the Holy Spirit. I was learning that the anointing is as powerful when conveyed through the word of authority into a camera as it is in the room. I determined that I would steward this lesson as faithfully as I could. On the third night I was due to speak on the subject of the Baptism with the Holy Spirit, so when the ministry time arrived I prophesied an outpouring of the Spirit to everyone watching at home on the TV, praying directly into the camera.

There was no way I could determine how many people might have received the Holy Spirit, but on my way to the airport the following day our party stopped at the home of a prominent government minister. In his house were a number of people waiting to see me including his sister in law. They had all been together watching the meeting on their TV the previous night. The sister in law testified that when I ministered to those watching on TV, the Holy Spirit came so powerfully into the living room that so she fell off her chair onto the floor, was baptized with the Holy Spirit and began speaking in tongues!

For me this was a very powerful lesson in growing in the ways of the Holy Spirit. I saw something new – that the anointing can be released through the medium of TV as powerfully as when physically present in the room. Since then I have ministered many times in that way, especially at LifeSpring Church services with our livestream facility. We regularly hear of testimonies of healing and breakthrough from people watching and receiving in their homes.

The point is this; the anointing is something we steward through wisdom. It is something in which we grow in our understanding. In this chapter we are going to explore how to walk and grow in the anointing. We could liken this to learning to drive a car – you are conscious of the power of the engine beneath the bonnet stretched out in front of you. But you have to learn to use the controls, read the instruments, observe your surroundings and navigate the road ahead. While all the time you are dependent on the car's engine to propel you forward.

I hope you will learn to lean into the wisdom of God to do what he has called and equipped you to do. None of us begin as experts. You must be willing to make mistakes and grow in your stewardship of the anointing. God understands that 'we have this treasure in earthen vessels' (2 Corinthians 4:7). He will do his part but he doesn't replace us. You have to play your part too.

The Goal is Ministry

The first priority is to ensure that the anointing doesn't simply remain as the anointing but translates into ministry. To be effective we need to understand the two are different.

> *. . . God anointed Jesus of Nazareth with the Holy Spirit and power, and how he went around doing good and healing all who were under the power of the devil, because God was with him.*
>
> Acts 10:38

God anointed Jesus with the Spirit and he began doing Holy Spirit works. We have seen that Jesus was anointed with the Holy Spirit at the river Jordan (Luke 3:21-22). Then he began his ministry (Luke 3:23). The goal of every anointing is the ministry of the Holy Spirit in the earth. This is exactly how it worked for Jesus and he is our model. There is no ministry without an anointing but an anointing doesn't guarantee a ministry. An anointing is not a ministry, but it can become a ministry through our cooperation with the Holy Spirit.

God's power is given for a purpose. Every believer should be anointed with the Holy Spirit and then every anointing should translate into ministry. There are many gifts, many operations of the Holy Spirit, but they are all intended to result in ministry. In this way Jesus is revealed to the world, broken lives become whole, lost souls are saved, sick bodies get healed. The kingdom of God comes in power on the earth.

Many believers want an anointing but they are not necessarily prepared to walk in obedience for the anointing to translate into ministry. The anointing alone will not save the world, but anointed ministry will. The anointing is the Holy Spirit's connection with you. Ministry is the Holy Spirit's connection with the needy. But it takes place through you. Anointing is what God does. Ministry is what you do. The sober fact is that you can die an anointed man or woman with your destiny still dormant and your anointing coiled up inside you unless you walk in obedience to God and connect his anointing with ministry.

Ministry is another way of saying 'serving the Lord in the power of the Spirit'. It is giving away what God has given you. We should make sure we are giving all the time. In the geography of the land of Israel the river Jordan flows into two seas, the Sea of Galilee and the Dead Sea. The Sea of Galilee is fresh and abundant with fish and marine life. The Dead Sea on the other hand is stagnant and salty, nothing can live in it. The cause of this contrast is simple – the Sea of Galilee has an inlet and an outlet. It receives and it gives. The Dead Sea on the other hand only receives, it gives nothing. It is a topographical picture of a life principle. If you want to remain fresh and fruitful, keep giving. Keep ministering. Keep serving in the power of the Holy Spirit.

It is evident that ministry is the focus of the New Testament. It was the goal of the disciples. It was the aim of the apostles.

It was the priority in Paul's mind. In Colossians 4:17 he gives this instruction to one of his team members, 'Tell Archipus to see that he fulfils his ministry'. To his spiritual son Timothy he simply says, 'Fulfil your ministry' (2 Timothy 4:5). Then in Acts 20 he says this to the Ephesian elders:

> *'But none of these things move me; nor do I count my life dear to myself, so that I may finish my race with joy,* ***and the ministry*** *which I received from the Lord Jesus, to testify to the gospel of the grace of God'*
>
> Acts 20:24

What is ministry? Ministry is work! Ministry is co-working with the Holy Spirit. It is a partnership with God. Ministry is work undertaken serving the interests of God and his kingdom.

> *And He Himself gave some to be apostles, some prophets, some evangelists, and some pastors and teachers, for the equipping of the saints* ***for the work of ministry****, for the edifying of the body of Christ.*
>
> Ephesians 4:11-12

So you see ministry is work given by God for you to do! An Old English word for the anointing is 'unction'. Unction is the power, but you need a function for your unction. It takes more than an anointing to be effective for Christ. The anointing must move within and through us to the needy. It is like the difference between potential and kinetic energy. A reservoir contains potential energy, a waterfall contains kinetic energy. A battery contains potential energy, the electricity that flows from it is kinetic energy. Anointing is like potential energy, ministry is like kinetic energy. God wants kinetic Christians. We have to turn the potential of anointing to the kinetic of ministry to see fruit.

A lot of believers are praying for a greater anointing without realizing that their reservoir is already full. They need instead to learn how to turn the power that God has given them into ministry. They need to turn their potential energy into kinetic energy. That is what we are going to explore now. I want to equip you with all the principles possible in order for you to increase and sustain a permanently anointed life. Praise God! What a prospect. It is entirely possible and God has planned this for you. Let's go!

Be a Holy Spirit landing strip

My first trip to Africa had as its destination the remote village of Tebalong in the mountainous kingdom of Lesotho. The first leg of our journey was an international flight to Johannesburg from where our second flight took us on to Maseru the capital of Lesotho. Our third flight was in a tiny 4 seater, single engine Cessna in which we flew high above the Drakensburg Mountains to our final destination. On arrival at Tebalong our pilot had one goal in mind – to locate the rough grass airstrip on the side of the mountain and safely bring us down. From my seat in the plane I could hardly believe we were actually going to land on the precarious strip of grass in front of us. But our pilot was from the Missionary Aviation Fellowship and these MAF pilots are some of the best in the world. Sure enough we made it safely.

The Holy Spirit is constantly on the look-out for suitable landing strips, men and women on whom he can 'touch down'. What is an outpouring of the Holy Spirit if nothing less than this? What is a revival if not God showing up in power among his people and through them to the world? Let me urge you to keep the fire of God burning in your life. Fan it into flame! Do not quench the Holy Spirit. Give God the best landing strip you can and you will attract his presence and power in ever greater measure.

Aaron and his sons

Now it is time to get really practical in our apprenticeship with the Holy Spirit. I am going to take a number of passages in the Old Covenant to illustrate how to learn and grow in the ways of the anointing of the Spirit.

> *And Aaron and his sons you shall bring to the door of the tabernacle of meeting, and you shall wash them with water. Then you shall take the garments, put the tunic on Aaron, and the robe of the ephod, the ephod, and the breastplate, and gird him with the intricately woven band of the ephod. You shall put the turban on his head, and put the holy crown on the turban. And you shall take the anointing oil, pour it on his head, and anoint him.*
>
> Exodus 29:4-7

Exodus chapters 28 and 29 contain a description of the anointing of Aaron the brother of Moses, and his sons, to the priesthood. It is in fact an instruction manual for how the anointing operates and how we can function practically in the Holy Spirit's power.

Aaron was chosen by God for the specific role he was to play in the same way that you and I are chosen to operate in certain gifts and ministries. The anointing is connected to the call of God. Aaron's anointing was connected to the call of God on his life to be high priest. He was not a priest with a prophet's anointing or a prophet with a king's anointing. He was a priest with the anointing of a priest. For every call there is an anointing. You are anointed to do what God called you to do.

When everything was prepared Aaron and his sons were separated, dressed for the moment, anointed with oil and finally deployed in the work or ministry they were assigned to. What we see is a divine order or procedure that the Holy Spirit was working to. It is found in several passages of the Law of Moses. Let's begin right here with this passage from Leviticus and highlight the lessons for us.

> *He who is the high priest among his brethren, on whose head the anointing oil was poured and who is consecrated to wear the garments, shall not uncover his head nor tear his clothes; nor shall he go near any dead body, nor defile himself for his father or his mother, nor profane the sanctuary of his God; for the consecration of the anointing oil of his God is upon him: I am the LORD.*
>
> Leviticus 21:10-12

God chooses whom He anoints

'He who is the high priest among his brethren . . .'

If you want to increase in your own anointing it is essential that you celebrate the anointing God has placed on others. One of the most important principles governing the anointing is the recognition that God does the choosing! Here's the point – God's choice might not be your choice. There may be many reasons why we question God's choice of those he anoints. In fact it takes considerable humility at times to simply receive some of God's anointed servants.

Notice that this Scripture says that God chose the High Priest, 'from among his brethren'. Accepting whom God chooses is made all the harder the more we know the person concerned or the closer we are to them. God anointed Jesus of Nazareth, 'from among his brothers', his family and his townsfolk. They all knew him – that was the problem, and they stumbled over the one from among them whom God had anointed.

> *When He had come to His own country, He taught them in their synagogue, so that they were astonished and said, "Where did this Man get this wisdom and these mighty works? Is this not the carpenter's son? Is not His mother called Mary? And His brothers James, Joses, Simon, and Judas? And His sisters, are they not all with us? Where then did this Man get all these things?" So they were offended at Him. But Jesus said to them, "A prophet is not without honor except in his own country and in his own house." Now He did not do many mighty works there because of their unbelief.*
>
> Matthew 13:54-58

The people failed to recognize Jesus as the Christ because they were so familiar with Jesus the carpenter's son. What should my response be when I see someone emerge from among my peer group with a greater anointing than myself or an anointing I wished I had? I should do all I can to celebrate them and cheer them on. We should never allow jealousy, offence or petty rivalry to discourage the grace of God on another person. The rejection that an anointed man or woman receives is frequently not from an enemy but from family or friends. Joseph suffered at the hands of his jealous brothers. David's anointing set him up for conflict with his brothers. If you want to grow in your own anointing make sure you honour the anointing on the life of others.

Get dressed for the anointing

'. . . who is consecrated to wear the garments . . .'

When you dress, you prepare for the occasion. We all dress for the moment in hand with our physical clothes; it should be no different with the anointing. It means we prepare ourselves accordingly. The high priest and his sons were given specific clothes to wear, appropriate to their office and anointing. So too, we dress ourselves in preparation for a life of anointed ministry. It is not God's responsibility to get you dressed. His responsibility is to anoint you once you are dressed. We have to clothe ourselves in preparation for the anointing. What are the clothes we should be dressing ourselves in for the anointing?

- Clothe yourself with humility – 1 Peter 5:5
- Clothe yourself with righteousness – Isaiah 61:10
- Clothe yourself with the armour of God – Ephesians 6:10
- Clothe yourself with love – Colossians 3:14
- Clothe yourself with praise – Isaiah 61:10

God is looking for those who diligently prepare themselves, expecting a mighty anointing for ministry. He has an anointing for you to carry into your daily life and specific ministry. Are you preparing? Are you walking in love? Are you living in praise and gratitude? Let's get dressed!

Pay the price for the anointing

'. . . shall not uncover his head nor tear his clothes; nor shall he go near any dead body . . .'

When the anointing of the Spirit is upon you there is a greater degree of responsibility to watch your life and guard your heart, because other people are affected. Let me explain. The regulation we see here had to do with the mourning for a dead family member. According to Numbers 19:11 it was actually the same requirement for all the people of Israel. The difference here was that if a regular member of the community defiled themselves it would only affect their family. Whereas if a priest was defiled it affected his ministry. He would not be able to function as a priest to the people.

If you do not guard the anointing that has been entrusted to you, make no mistake about it, others are affected, others loose out. Therefore the Holy Spirit has prior claim upon your life. What may be OK for others is not OK for you! Personal feelings, preferences and priorities have to be laid to one side. Even innocent leisure activities and socializing come under greater scrutiny because the anointed servant is on constant duty. The anointing comes first. We dare not violate this priority.

When a leader falls morally or they are taken out of ministry because of wrong-doing, we rightfully mourn the fact – but we don't always consider what future blessings have been stolen from all the people who will no longer receive from that ministry. The good news is that God is in the business of restoration. Just as a priest who was defiled could be brought back into ministry, we need to enable fallen leaders to be restored because it is the anointing that needs to be recovered not just the minister!

Stay under the anointing

'. . . nor shall he go out of the sanctuary . . .'

When the Holy Spirit is moving we have to learn how to stay in step with him. When God's Spirit rests upon you, learn to remain under the consciousness of his presence. All the time God is moving, move with him. In this passage we see this principle powerfully portrayed. The Lord says to the priests through Moses, that they should continue to remain in the sanctuary throughout the time that is required of them because the anointing oil is upon them. This is especially true when operating in a spiritual gift. If the prophetic Spirit is present in the room, keep prophesying until he has finished. If there is a healing anointing flowing, keep laying on hands, keep ministering regardless of your personal comfort or convenience.

> *In those days, the multitude being very great and having nothing to eat, Jesus called His disciples to Him and said to them, "I have compassion on the multitude, because they have now continued with me three days and have nothing to eat.*
>
> Mark 8:1-2

On the occasion quoted here Jesus ministered to the people for three days without a break. Can you imagine that! It must have been like heaven on earth. Time itself was suspended and the people were supernaturally sustained under the presence of the Holy Spirit operating in Jesus. He didn't cut out, he remained in that anointing all the time it operated through him. There were times recorded in the gospels when the Holy Spirit was moving so powerfully no one dare move! This is how Jesus operated in his ministry.

> *And He came down with them and stood on a level place with a crowd of His disciples and a great multitude of people from all Judea and Jerusalem, and from the seacoast of Tyre and Sidon, who came to hear Him and be healed of their diseases, as well*

as those who were tormented with unclean spirits. And they were healed. And the whole multitude sought to touch Him, for power went out from Him and healed them all.

Luke 6:17-19

Our friend Isobel Skullasen was preaching on one occasion and the people who had gathered there all came hoping to receive a prophetic word. The pastor convening the meeting promised the people they would all receive. Isobel had not been consulted on this but the Lord gave her the instruction to go ahead – there was only one problem – there were hundreds of people present. She began prophesying around 10.00pm and continued without a break until 6.00am the following morning. The anointing strengthened her and every single person received!

We live in an age of instant everything. What was once classified as 'fast food' is now the benchmark. No one wants to wait for anything. But God is not like that. We have to learn to remain when God is moving whether it disrupts our plans and agendas or not. There is no need to hurry away when you have received prayer in a ministry line; stay where you are and keep receiving.

The nature of the anointing

We are now going to look at another passage from the Old Covenant to discover the very nature and character of the anointing.

Moreover the LORD spoke to Moses, saying: "Also take for yourself quality spices – five hundred shekels of liquid myrrh, half as much sweet-smelling

> *cinnamon (two hundred and fifty shekels), two hundred and fifty shekels of sweet-smelling cane, five hundred shekels of cassia, according to the shekel of the sanctuary, and a hin of olive oil. And you shall make from these a holy anointing oil, an ointment compounded according to the art of the perfumer. It shall be a holy anointing oil.*
>
> Exodus 30:22-25

God gave to Moses very precise instructions as to how the anointing oil was to be composed. Its appearance, its feel, its fragrance – they were all the result of a very specific recipe. This oil was used to anoint Aaron and his sons and is symbolic of the Holy Spirit so the composition is significant.

The anointing is authentic

The oil used for the purpose of anointing was crafted by a perfumer! It was not like cooking oil, plain and functional. It had the most beautiful aroma. This is no accident. It is a description of the Holy Spirit. This is what his presence is likened to – a perfume! When a person is living under the anointing they smell like heaven.

The ingredients of the anointing oil were liquid myrrh, sweet smelling cinnamon, sweet smelling cane and cassia. These were added to the base ingredient of olive oil. Concerning this oil God said, '. . . nor shall you make any other like it, according to its composition' (verse 32). The anointing is absolutely genuine and unique. It comes from heaven. It has a divine composition. It is not measured by outward signs and manifestations. These may occur but they are simply responses to the presence of the Holy Spirit, they are not the anointing itself. You can't operate in the Holy Spirit simply by imitating what others do. It has to be the real thing.

I am sure we have all seen displays of personality, drama or attempts to get a result by imitating what others have done. This should not dampen our quest for the real thing. A fake only proves the existence of the genuine, it does not disprove it. If we guard our heart at all times God will be faithful. If we don't sense the presence of the Holy Spirit at any time, make that an opportunity to draw ever closer to him and his time his presence will be manifest.

The anointing is holy

'. . . And you shall make from these a holy anointing oil . . .'

When you experience the genuine anointing of the Holy Spirit you touch the holiness of God. It is not something to take casually. Whether you really understand this or not, the anointing of the Holy Spirit sets you apart. We just cannot get away from the issue of separation to God! The principle of separation means we set ourselves apart to God and his Holy Spirit from anything and everything that is questionable. You will fear to sin. Your spiritual senses will become highly tuned. Your heart will be sensitized.

The process of preparation for Aaron and his sons into their priesthood was meticulous. God was not slap-dash and careless with his anointing. You and I are meant to represent the Holy Spirit who anoints us. When we think of the Holy Spirit coming in the form of a dove and alighting on the shoulder of Jesus we should immediately ask the question, 'How do you walk with a dove?' You should do everything possible not to upset that dove. Paul says, 'And do not grieve the Holy Spirit of God, by whom you were sealed for the day of redemption' (Ephesians 4:30).

The anointing is fragrant

'. . . an ointment compounded according to the art of the perfumer.'

The presence and anointing of the Holy Spirit is sweet and attractive, not jarring and harsh. It is a contradiction for a person to minister the sweet presence of the Spirit while at the same time being forceful, brash or drawing attention to themselves. The Holy Spirit does not force anyone to behave in strange or confusing ways. He does not violate our conscience or our faith.

I want you to notice that expression, 'the art of the perfumer'. God is a divine perfumer, and he has composed the anointing to be the most attractive and beautiful perfume you could imagine. We may not understand everything the Holy Spirit instructs a person to do but if it is genuinely the Holy Spirit, we can be sure of two things. First the life of the person under the anointing will be filled with love and the fruit of the Spirit. Secondly, the result of their words and actions will be love, joy and peace.

The Result is the Glory of God

The final chapter of Exodus describes what happened when the Tabernacle had been constructed, the items of furniture placed inside, the priests took their positions and finally everything was anointed for its use to God.

> *Then the cloud covered the tabernacle of meeting, and the glory of the LORD filled the tabernacle. And Moses was not able to enter the tabernacle of meeting, because the cloud rested above it, and the glory of the LORD filled the tabernacle.*
>
> Exodus 40:34-35

The ultimate aim of the anointing is the manifestation of God's glory in the earth. Under the Old Covenant, God filled the physical house of the Tabernacle. His glory came down and dwelt with his people. In the New Covenant God filled the temple of his Son Jesus. He came to reveal the Father to the world, he manifest the glory of God through his life when the Holy Spirit came upon him, not before. But it didn't end with his Son. Jesus is the model for what the Father wants to do through his people the church.

After his return to the Father, Jesus poured out the Holy Spirit on the temple of his church, a multi-membered body, filled with the Holy Spirit and manifesting his glory to the world. When a man or woman is living in the anointing, it is God who gets the glory and God who reveals his glory through that man or woman. We are the vessels and channels of the glory of God. The day must come when the earth witnesses the revealing of God's glory through his anointed people. Let us pray for this, strive for this and yield our hearts to the Spirit of God to see this take place in our lives.

Appendix:

Christ – prophet, priest and king

In the Old Covenant God raised up men and women who were anointed with the Holy Spirit to deliver his people from their enemies and exercise leadership over them. These were the judges. They were a unique set of people and ministered in a unique period of time. We looked in particular at Othniel and Samson as examples of this. But the judges were not the only ones to have exercised an anointed ministry. There is another class of people who occupied offices appointed by God; namely the prophets, the priests and the kings. They were all commissioned by the anointing of oil, symbolic of the Holy Spirit's choice and empowerment and to varying degrees they experienced the power of the Holy Spirit in the exercise of their ministries.

Although priests and prophets existed prior to the period of the judges, with the emergence of the kings of Israel, the offices of prophet, priest and king are established as a complete class of ministries. There is even an interesting overlap of sorts at the end of the period of the judges. Samuel was both a prophet and a judge. He led the people of Israel to victory over the Philistines, he judged the people, travelling on a circuit around the nation and he operated in the office of prophet (1 Samuel 7:15). There was also Eli who ministered as a priest but who also served as a judge for the people of Israel for forty years (1 Samuel 4:18).

No one individual in the Old Testament combines all three offices although there are certain outstanding individuals who come close in some ways. David was anointed to the office of king, but also carried a powerful prophetic anointing. Peter, in his message on the Day of Pentecost even refers to him as a prophet (Acts 2:30). Then there is the fascinating person of Melchizedek, who is described as 'king of Salem (later to become Jerusalem) and priest of God most high' (Hebrews 7:1).

Prophecies in the Old Covenant indicate that when God's messiah appeared he would fulfil these three ministries in himself. This is exactly what we see in the person of Jesus of Nazareth. He embodied all three offices and exercised all three in his ministry. This teaching is referred to as the three-fold office of Christ and has been recognised by Christians from a wide range of backgrounds for hundreds of years. Indeed this has been taught by the Roman Catholic Church as well as classic reformers like Eusebius and Calvin right up to modern day.

The ministries of prophets, priests and kings each represented an aspect of Jesus' own anointed ministry and how he would defeat his enemy Satan. The three-fold office of Christ is a lens through which we can view the nature of the anointing of the Holy Spirit, how it operated in the person of Jesus the Son of God and then in the church his body. To understand how these anointed ministries developed we first need to go back to the book of Genesis.

First Covenant Anointings

> *So the LORD God said to the serpent: "Because you have done this, you are cursed more than all cattle, and more than every beast of the field; on your belly you shall go, and you shall eat dust all the days of your life. And I will put enmity between you and the*

woman, and between your seed and her Seed; he shall bruise your head, and you shall bruise His heel."

Genesis 3:14-15

Genesis 3:15 reveals that God would raise up a deliverer or messiah from the womb of Eve who would crush the head of Satan, rescue mankind from his power and restore his original creation purpose for the human race. From that point on there was as it were, a contract on Satan's head – and he knew it. His activity had a time limit. He would be forever on the lookout for who this deliverer might be and from where he would appear.

Initially Satan had to watch everywhere for the emergence of the messiah. But this changed with the calling of Abram. When God chose Abram and his offspring as his instruments in the earth, Satan's focus narrowed down to the Jewish race and so through the long line of bible history we see Satan's continued persecution of the Jewish people. Whenever there was even the hint of a possibility that a deliverer might appear, the devil sought to destroy him. The killing of babies by Pharaoh; the plot of Haman to destroy the Jewish people at the time of Esther and Herod's killing of the infants in Bethlehem are all examples.

Finally however, Jesus of Nazareth walked onto the stage of history. He was baptized by John and anointed with the Holy Spirit by the Father. He lived and ministered under that anointing, a prophetic anointing, a priestly anointing and a kingly anointing. Each of these offices was anticipated in their Old Covenant form first.

Prophet

Moses was an incredible prophet of God. But during his final instruction to the people of Israel, as they prepared to cross the

Jordan River, God revealed to Moses that he would raise up one greater than him.

> *The LORD your God will raise up for you a prophet like me from your midst, from your brethren. Him you shall hear, according to all you desired of the LORD your God in Horeb in the day of the assembly, saying, "Let me not hear again the voice of the LORD my God, nor let me see this great fire anymore, lest I die."*
>
> Deuteronomy 18:15-16

The promise of a prophet was part of the messiah anointing that Jesus would fulfil. Jesus came as the ultimate prophetic voice to the world. The Book of Hebrews states, 'In these last days God has spoken to us through his Son' (Hebrews 1:2). He is the living eternal Word, the logos of God. He existed in the beginning with God and in the fullness of time appeared in human form, the word made flesh. In Acts 3:22-24 Peter refers directly to this passage in Deuteronomy as being fulfilled in Jesus. Furthermore, Jesus' miracle works were added evidence of his prophetic ministry (Luke 7:16, 24:19).

In what ways was Jesus a prophet like Moses?

- Moses mediated the Old Covenant. Jesus mediated the New Covenant.
- Moses brought a revelation from God. Jesus brought the ultimate revelation of God.
- Moses led the people of Israel out of bondage and into their salvation. Jesus came to deliver us from the power of sin and Satan and set us free.
- Moses' ministry was accompanied by supernatural signs and wonders as was Jesus' own ministry.

It is evident that Jesus did not come to bring an end to prophetic ministry, rather he is the Word itself made flesh, the pinnacle of everything God wanted to say. Then the prophetic anointing that was on Jesus was transmitted to the church on the Day of Pentecost. In Joel's prophecy concerning the outpouring of the Holy Spirit God says, 'your sons and your daughters shall prophesy' (Joel 2:28). Prophecy is a regular feature of the early church and Paul normalizes its presence through his teaching in 1 Corinthians 12 and 14. The body of Christ includes the function of speaking, it has a mouth! Jehovah is a speaking God and his people are his mouthpiece. The ministry of Elijah and Elisha powerfully portrays this divine handover of the prophetic anointing of Christ to his church.

> *And so it was, when they had crossed over, that Elijah said to Elisha, "Ask! What may I do for you, before I am taken away from you?" Elisha said, "Please let a double portion of your spirit be upon me." So he said, "You have asked a hard thing. Nevertheless, if you see me when I am taken from you, it shall be so for you; but if not, it shall not be so." Then it happened, as they continued on and talked, that suddenly a chariot of fire appeared with horses of fire, and separated the two of them; and Elijah went up by a whirlwind into heaven.*
>
> 2 Kings 2:9-11

In this passage Elijah is a prophetic type of Jesus and Elisha of the church. Elijah ascended to heaven and the Holy Spirit descended upon Elisha with a 'double anointing', Jesus was taken up to his Father and the Holy Spirit fell on the gathered disciples on the Day of Pentecost. Elisha asked for and expected to receive the anointing that was on his master Elijah and he ministered in a greater anointing than Elijah.

> *Now when the sons of the prophets who were from Jericho saw him, they said, "The spirit of Elijah rests on Elisha." And they came to meet him, and bowed to the ground before him.*
>
> 2 Kings 2:15

There are many parallels; Elisha followed Elijah as his disciple. Elisha ministered in the same Spirit as Elijah and now the church receives the same Spirit as Jesus. The church is a prophetic voice and has received a prophetic anointing. But the prophetic anointing in the church is not limited to prophesying only. We also recognize the New Covenant office of the prophet and this is taught explicitly in the New Testament (Ephesians 2:20, 4:11). We have every right to expect God to raise up prophets among us and we should rejoice and recognize their ministry today.

Finally the body of Christ is God's prophetic people. It is not simply that individuals may prophesy or that the office of the prophet functions in the church – wonderful though these things are. But more than that, the body of Christ herself speaks prophetically in her conduct, words and very presence in the world. We stand out. We are different. We swim against the tide of this world. We represent another kingdom, we belong to another world.

Priest

Toward the end of the time of the judges, a man named Eli occupied the office of High Priest to the people of Israel, ministering with his two sons at the tabernacle where it was kept in the town of Shiloh. It was under Eli's care that the prophet Samuel grew up from an early age. Eli was an ungodly man who allowed his sons to commit the most terrible crimes of corruption right under his nose, doing nothing to restrain them. We are all familiar with the story of the young Samuel hearing the voice of God and running to Eli thinking it was Eli who was calling him. We are not so familiar with the word that God brought through Samuel at that time, warning Eli of his wrong doing and declaring that he would raise up another priest in his place.

> *Then I will raise up for myself a faithful priest who shall do according to what is in my heart and in my mind. I will build him a sure house, and he shall walk before my anointed forever.*
>
> 1 Samuel 2:35

Eli failed to represent God's interests and God pronounced judgment against him. But more than that, the whole priesthood of Aaron, from which Eli came, was destined to be replaced by Christ, our eternal great High Priest. Jesus did not come from the priestly tribe of Levi but from the tribe of Judah. It was a completely different order of priesthood. We can see from Psalm 110 and Hebrew 7 that Jesus came as a priest after the order of Melchizedek.

> *The LORD has sworn and will not relent, "You are a priest forever according to the order of Melchizedek."*
>
> Psalms 110:4

As our great high priest Jesus offered the ultimate sacrifice to God, his own body. He did this willingly, he chose to lay down his life for us. This was a mutual act of love between the Father and the Son. Jesus took our place at the cross in a vicarious, priestly sacrifice and now he represents us before the Father in heaven in his priestly ministry there.

> *For we do not have a High Priest who cannot sympathize with our weaknesses, but was in all points tempted as we are, yet without sin. Let us therefore come boldly to the throne of grace that we may obtain mercy and find grace to help in time of need.*
>
> Hebrews 4:15-16

As our great high priest, Jesus is both fully man and fully God. He stands between us and the Father, making intercession for us. There can only be one Jesus, who died for our sins and lives to mediate for us before the Father. However, the priesthood of Melchizedek does not stop with Christ. The church is a priesthood of all believers. Look at how Peter describes God's people – taking this same expression from Exodus 19 where God refers to his people as a 'royal priesthood and a holy nation' (verse 6).

> *But you are a chosen generation, a royal priesthood, a holy nation, His own special people, that you may proclaim the praises of Him who called you out of darkness into His marvelous light; who once were not a people but are now the people of God, who had not obtained mercy but now have obtained mercy.*
>
> 1 Peter 2:9-10

John also refers to the church as 'priests to our God' (Revelation 1:6). Our anointing as priests is not in any sense to mediate for our sins – only Jesus could do that. But it is real none the less. In what way?

- In the offering of spiritual sacrifices to God

The offering or our praise, worship and prayer is the first and foremost way the priestly ministry of the church on earth is exercised.

> *Ye also, as lively stones, are built up a spiritual house, a holy priesthood, to offer up spiritual sacrifices, acceptable to God by Jesus Christ.*
>
> 1 Peter 2:5

- In the preaching of the gospel

Look at how Paul describes the preaching of the gospel to the Gentiles as a priestly ministry:

> *But on some points I have written to you very boldly by way of reminder, because of the grace given me by God to be a minister of Christ Jesus to the Gentiles in* ***the priestly service of the gospel of God****, so that the offering of the Gentiles may be acceptable, sanctified by the Holy Spirit.*
>
> Romans 15:15-16 ESV

There is nothing more mediatory than standing before people as God's representatives, sharing the good news of the gospel and calling them to repentance and faith.

- In declaring the blessings of God

> *Speak unto Aaron and unto his sons, saying, on this wise ye shall bless the children of Israel, saying unto them . . .*
>
> Numbers 6:23

If a central role of the Old Covenant priest was to bless the people, how much more so for the New Covenant priesthood! The one who blesses exercises spiritual authority. Blessing empowers you, equips you and fortifies you. We are even commanded to bless our enemies and those who curse us

(Matthew 5:44, Luke 6:28). Words of blessing are carriers of life and power to God's people, our communities and our cities. We are called to bless.

King

One of King David's great longings was to build a house for his God, a permanent place of worship to replace the tabernacle. He shared this desire with the prophet Nathan who initially supported it. Then God spoke to Nathan, bringing adjustment to David's ambition. David was not to build such a temple, he had been a man of warfare, a man of blood. However one of his sons would instead build a house for God. This prophecy has a double level of fulfilment for although Solomon built the literal temple in Jerusalem, another son of David would emerge as king, to build a spiritual house for God.

> *When your days are fulfilled and you rest with your fathers, I will set up your seed after you, who will come from your body, and I will establish his kingdom. He shall build a house for my name, and I will establish the throne of his kingdom forever.*
>
> 2 Samuel 7:12-13

It was clearly understood that this prophecy could only be fulfilled in the anointed messiah and no surprise that those who recognized Jesus as the Christ referred to him as 'the Son of David' (Matthew 12:23, 21:9).

King David was indeed the closest representation of God's kingdom on earth prior to Christ. God himself described David as 'a man after my own heart' (1 Samuel 13:14). He served God's purpose with passion, led his people with humility and fought God's battles with courage. He was human and made some terrible mistakes but nevertheless God identified himself with David like no other before or after and made a covenant with him.

Most significantly David was anointed by the Holy Spirit! At the young age of 17 he was discovered by the prophet Samuel who poured the anointing oil on his head and from that day the Spirit of God came upon him in power (1 Samuel 16:13). It would be many years until David finally occupied the throne in Jerusalem and was anointed again in recognition of this office. There was no one like David.

Jesus came to introduce the kingdom of God into the earth. He announced the presence of the kingdom, called men and women to enter the kingdom through repentance and he manifest kingdom power in signs and miracles. All of this demonstrated that his kingdom was not an earthly kingdom but one that began with the willing submission of men and women to the will of God.

Having paid the price for sin and risen from the dead, God has exalted him to the highest place heaven can afford. He now reigns from heaven, extending his kingdom on the earth through his people and preparing everything for the time of his kingly return to claim the earth as rightfully his. Jesus made it clear that his kingdom had been passed across from the natural people of David, the Jews, to a New Covenant people who would bear its fruit (Matthew 21:43).

The church, Christ's body has been called to rule and reign in life in Christ. We are a royal priesthood, a holy nation, God's own people. Sharing in Christ's reign in this life is all part of fulfilling the kingly anointing that was on Christ and now rests upon us. Through the kingly anointing, redeemed men and women are restored to God's original purpose of representing him in the earth. There is no place for victimhood or defeat. The people of God reign in Christ despite the presence of Satanic opposition in the world. They reign in life and they reign in death. God's people are the living testimony to the enduring power of God's kingdom present in the earth and through them God's kingdom grows and expands until Christ returns.

Other books by Tony Wastall:

Your Word is Your World

Win the World or Escape the Earth

From Home to the Throne

Tithing Today

How to Come Back Strong

Maturity Matters

Thy Kingdom Come

To purchase these and other materials and for more information on Tony Wastall and LifeSpring Ministries connect with us via **www.lifespring.uk.com**

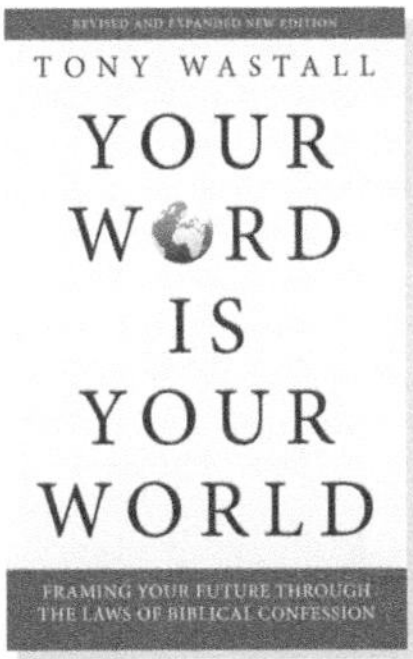